REJECTION to ACCEPTANCE
57 Poems That Finally Made It

REJECTION to ACCEPTANCE
57 Poems That Finally Made It

by

Patricia Williams

© 2023 Patricia Williams. All rights reserved.
This material may not be reproduced in any form, published,
reprinted, recorded, performed, broadcast,
rewritten or redistributed without
the explicit permission of Patricia Williams.
All such actions are strictly prohibited by law.

Cover image from Microsoft 365 free stock image
Photo of author by Patricia Williams

ISBN: 978-1-63980-321-7

Kelsay Books
502 South 1040 East, A-119
American Fork, Utah 84003
Kelsaybooks.com

*I wish to thank all of the friends and family
who listened to my poems, especially
the Waupaca Writers group
and Keith who was there at the beginning.*

Introduction

This is not a book about "How to Write Poetry," there is an abundance of those. *This is a memoire, an account of one poet's journey* with notes and comments on each poem's back story, from initial inspiration to its ultimate publication, an interaction between reader and writer. It's a book about 57 rejected poems that finally "made it" to publication.

People of all ages, not just poets, but readers of poetry, new poets as well as writers with some experience, those wishing to start something new, writing groups, students in classrooms and attending workshops, will all find something here.

This is a look behind the scenes—it uncovers things that readers don't usually see. Notes appear after each poem and address my experience with submitting work to literary journals. Back stories include sources of inspiration, feedback from readers and coaches, the number of rejections each poem received, editors' remarks and other pertinent items. These poems were all finally published, often after five, six, seven or more, rejections.

The poem's histories, 1) are a vehicle for critique and group discussion, 2) promote an understanding of the submission process, and 3) *perhaps most important,* support conversation on the need for persistence, the fear of failure, and how we define success.

Contents

One Poet's Journey   13

PART I Going Places: Here, There & Everywhere

Counting Cats	24
Wayfarers	26
No Photosynthesis Occurs	28
Lyon Gastronomique	30
Lorca's *Duende*	32
Sketches Along the Yangtze	34
Ethereal Collision	36
Impermanence	38
Thoughts of Alfred's World	40
Traveling	42
Essaouira*	44
The Saints Said Nothing	46
Dancing *Flamenco* in Ronda	48
Expatriate	50

PART II Of Things Social: Principles & Opinions

There Goes the Neighborhood	54
Remembering Emmet Till	56
Midterm Blossoms, 2018	58
I Deal with "The Problem"	60
Life in a Word	62
I Listen to Gorecki's Symphony*	64
Praise Paper and Red Tape	66
Feral Tenacity	68

PART III Nature: trees, the sky, some fur & some feathers

The Breadcrumb Plate	72
Villanelle for the Birch: An Arboreal Romance	74
Home Sweet Home Concerto	76
Night Comes	78
Magic in Collapsing Stars	80
Magic Evenings	82
Midnight Encounter	84
Some Things Die Before Called	86
Wait 'til Tomorrow	88
Winter Sunlight	90
Insomnia	92
Whiteout Report	94
In Praise of Challenging Cycles	96
Elegy Before Snow Falls	98
Night Music	100

PART IV Humor: Not Only Light Verse,
  But Also Ironic, Satirical

Juvenal Knew About Suffering	104
Land of the Lost: Unmatched Performance	106
Carpe Diem—Seize the Day	108
Never Know What You'll See in Wisconsin	110
Close Encounters: I Met Lassie on the Stage of the Oriental Theater in Chicago	112
Distress Signal: Growing Tomatoes Upside Down	114
Futile Struggle: Salute to the Rural Mailbox	116
Lockdown Is Frying My Brain	118
Waiting for Janis Joplin	120

PART V Home & Neighborhood: Coming & Going

Exiled	124
Islands	126
Homage to Art: Abstract and Conceptual	128
Lumber Business	130
Remembering Small Times	132
Door County Picnic	134
Family Legacy	136
Aunt Mae's Player Piano	138
Ahead of Schedule	140
Missing Home	142
All Hail Wausau, Wisconsin	144

One Poet's Journey

Most poets begin their craft at an early age—I began writing poems after retiring from a 32-year teaching career in Art and Design. Retirement didn't mean doing nothing. It was not a time to settle into "old age," as Dylan Thomas said, not time to "go gently," but a time "to rage." For me, "rage" meant to challenge, to take on something new.

I wrote academic papers as a university professor but had no experience with creative writing. I had a late start in college—began my bachelor's degree with two children and received my PhD after a third was born. That's another story.

A project I worked on before retiring required the translation of poems and inscriptions written in classical Chinese. My translator, Xixi Meng, felt the English interpretation I made from her literal translation was not only accurate, but as aesthetically pleasing as the original Chinese poetry. Her appraisal encouraged me to write poems of my own. Poetry & Art Editor F.J. Bergman, of *Mobius Magazine,* states she *"has no academic literary qualifications, but hangs out sometimes with people who do."* That also describes me.

So I played "catch-up" after I retired—designed my own poetry-writing program—read a lot, attended writer's workshops, familiarized myself with poetry publishing, joined my state poetry society, attended the conferences, subscribed to writer's magazines and joined a local writer's group. I took an online poetry-writing course, worked with several coaches and began to submit my poems to both online and print literary journals.

One of the things I came to appreciate about creative writing was how much poetry has in common with the pictorial arts. Both draw on the same principles of art and design. Although not necessarily using all of the principles in a single piece, composing poems, paintings and photographs requires using contrast, balance, focal point, repetition, rhythm, unity and variety. Poetry is painting with words, painting is visual poetry. Both elicit emotional responses.

About Inspiration

In the *Introduction* to this book, I stated that it is not about "How to Write Poetry" but I do give examples of situations that inspired my work. They may or may not stimulate someone else. Some poets say "the Muse" has deserted them, or they are waiting for her to "strike." Inhale your surroundings, inspiration is all around. It comes from experiences in both the human-created world and the world of nature.

There are no rules. Words don't magically descend from above in full sentences—follow a fly or bake a cake—inspiration is everywhere. I have occasionally started writing something that took on a life of its own. It doesn't happen to me often, but when it does, the poem almost writes itself. I can't tell you how it happens; it just does. Some examples are cited in the pages that follow.

Submitting and Rewriting

There may be poets who score a win on the first try, but the rejection notices I received could have wall-papered my whole house. To be a *traditionally published* poet or writer, a person must prepare to receive many more rejections than acceptances.

Call it "thick skin" or "stubbornness," determination and persistence kept me writing, revising and submitting, and revising, and submitting. I can't quantify the number of re-writes needed. Sometimes a little tweaking is enough, sometimes it takes several total rewrites. It helps to have other writers read your work, even if they write in a different genre.

I have ten years of modest success at this writing, with over three-hundred poems published in a variety of literary journals and other places. This includes a twenty-seven-poem chapbook, *The Port Side of Shadows—Poems of Travel* (Finishing Line Press, 2017) a sixty-poem collection *Midwest Medley* (Kelsay Books, 2018), and this book. I have also won a few awards.

Declined, Denied—*Rejected?*

Even seasoned, lifelong poets can be sensitive to the word "rejected." I was attending a conference and having a conversation with a well-published poet. I mentioned that a certain journal *rejected* my submission, the fifth one to say "no thanks" to a poem I had written. This successful poet visibly cringed, blood drained from her face and she uttered, *"Oh don't say THAT WORD!!"* (It's safer to use the word "declined" or "refused" when in the company of poets and writers). My advice? Get over it.

Competition is fierce in the literary field. Notices from publishers, a "reject" or "accept" of your work, can take six months or more. Some experts advise that you're not submitting enough if you're not getting rejections. Poets, it's said, should aim for a hundred rejections a year . . . really?

I am told that top-rated journals publish less than one percent of what they receive. Stories about inexperienced writers who submit poems and stories to elite magazines are often dismal. Some are emotionally crushed when rejected and never again submit work to any publication. Editors have personal preferences and journals have specialties. My advice? Take rejection letters in stride, re-evaluate your work, continue reading, writing and submitting.

Editor's Choice: Accept or Reject

A "reader" is a person in a publishing house who reads work directly from "the slush pile," slang for a stack of unsolicited work submitted to a publisher for consideration, a process also known as "weeding out." The reader makes judgements as to the suitability and quality of the work sent in. If the readers see it as a possibility, they forward it on to second readers or the editors.

The basic selection process works this way: *first readers* decide what will *not* be published, often reading only the first few lines, cutting out a large percentage of the total submissions. A second, more experienced reader group whittles that down further, again weeding out what seems unsuitable for their publication. The editor reads what is left. In small magazine and journal publishing, the editor and an assistant may do all the sorting. In contests, a small group, five to ten contenders, are sent to the final judge who makes the prize selections.

Many factors determine which work is accepted. A certain poem may not be the right fit for a particular journal, which doesn't mean the poem isn't good. A rejection may have nothing to do with the quality of the work. Aspiring writers need to read the journals to which they plan to submit. This may seem obvious, but inexperienced writers and poets don't always investigate which journals publish the kind of work they write.

The number of submissions a publisher receives for an issue is a matter beyond the poets' control. When they receive too many similar poems, editors are faced with making arbitrary choices. They can't always publish everything they like.

Personal Taste

Personal preference influences editors. With no rules, no concrete right or wrong in the creative fields, work rejected by one editor can be another's favorite piece. It has to appeal to the editors—the choices are subjective. No license is required to be an editor, no tests to pass; wounding someone's feelings isn't against the law.

Different experiences and background knowledge between writer and editors means that each may perceive and interpret the poems differently. All of the information and experiences a person accumulates, people and places, books read, music, etc. is their *schema* or background knowledge, a personal blueprint, used to validate what is being judged. Everyone has a unique schema.

When asked to define a good poem, Howard Moss, poetry editor of the prestigious *New Yorker* for forty years, replied, *"One I like."* David M. Harris, founding editor of *Rat's Ass Review* said, *"A good poem isn't one that gets the grades for following particular rules . . . not even sure I'm looking for good poems. I'm looking for MY kind of poems."*—*de gustibus non est disputandum*—you can't argue with taste.

I received an Editor's Award accompanied by a fifty-dollar check after four years of writing—which almost knocked me over. This was validation from an editor, my work appreciated and acknowledged. Speaking of money, most poets don't make any. They do something else to pay the bills. Many caution that if you want fame and fortune there are more promising places to get it. When you do receive payment, it can come in various forms: I once traded two of my books for a bottle of sparkling wine. I'm not sure who got the better deal.

They Disappear

An unfortunate, but fairly common occurrence is small literary journals closing down, cursed by lack of funding. Many are part of university and college departments who find they must cut funding, even though the staff is often composed of volunteers seeking experience in the publishing world.

Independent magazines funded by individuals also regularly close down, affected by the same malady: lack of funds. Several small presses that published my poems have closed during the ten years I have been writing. These very journals are the places where new voices are given a chance to be heard. When only large, well-established publishing houses exist, the literary world suffers.

Style, Fashion, Technology

Creative writing is subject to fashion and style, factors sometimes used in deciding which piece to accept. Notice that poetry found in today's top journals seldom uses end rhyme, though some say it's making a comeback. Also, the first word of each line is not usually capitalized unless it is the first word in a sentence. These devices, both having practical origins, are less used today because of new technology and cultural change. Bards once recited stories for the generally illiterate public. Rhyming verses were a way for both poet and audience to remember the words more easily, as it is with nursery rhymes. Capitalizing the first letter of each line is related to obsolete typesetting techniques.

I was attending a workshop session conducted by a well-known poet. She stiffened while rifling through a pile of the attendee's papers, and through clenched teeth, said, *"You NEVER capitalize the first word of every line! You capitalize only the first word in a sentence. PERIOD!"* She, as well as some others, consider such practices old-fashioned, obsolete, akin to wearing grandmother's dresses and speaking in Old English. Again, the editor's taste is final. Poetry today has no fixed rules.

Publishing a Book

When poets have written enough poems, some published, some not, they might assemble a manuscript, either a chapbook (usually 15–25 poems) or a collection (40–90 poems) arranged around a theme. Then starts the process of finding a publisher.

Traditional publishers often charge a small reading fee which doesn't guarantee they will accept your manuscript. If they do accept, they don't charge for their services—editing fees, proof-reading, cover design, formatting, printing, etc. Authors are sometimes asked to participate in marketing (give readings, for example) but marketing of the book is also done by the publishers.

Frustrated by rejections and lured by the promise of fame and high royalties, poets may choose to by-pass traditional publishers and use a "self-publish" service for their book. The self-published author, although assured publication, must take on the duties and expenses that are borne by a traditional publisher.

Some poets frustrated with traditional publishing wish to avoid the tasks associated with self-publishing and turn to what is derisively called "vanity publishers." These business' state that if they choose to publish your book, they will do everything (and, of course, charge for all services). Former U.S. Poet Laureate and Pulitzer Prize winner, Ted Kooser, summed it up in his book, *Writing Free & Brave:* "*The vanity press's basic criterion in selecting manuscripts to publish is whether or not your check bounces.*"

Many traditional publishers require a percentage of the poems in a manuscript to be previously published, a sort of screening process which assures the publisher that other professionals viewed at least some of the work as deserving publication. I knew that if I was going to write a book, I had a lot of submitting and portfolio-building to do.

Contests

There is no shortage of poetry contests, some for a single poem, some for an entire manuscript. Many journals and literary groups sponsor writing contests, usually with entry fees, although some are free. After three years of writing, submitting poems to journals, entering a few contests, receiving rejections but at times, being published, I entered the *Finishing Line Press,* "New Women's Voices" chapbook contest.

In addition to the top winners, ten more manuscripts would be selected, published and included in the regular catalog. Authors would also receive five free copies of the book. The entry fee wasn't high, but with no age or geographical restrictions, there would be a lot of competition. Nonetheless, three top winners plus ten others chosen for publication, seemed like decent odds.

My twenty-seven-poem chapbook, "The Portside of Shadows—Poems of Travel," was not a top winner, but was chosen to be published: *"The editors have selected your chapbook manuscript for publication in our general catalog. We had many excellent manuscripts to choose from but only our top entries were selected for publication. Congratulations."* I received the free books, an author's discount on additional books, a copyright, an Amazon listing and my book is in the *Finishing Line* catalog.

A Full Collection

Five years after writing my first poem, I assembled a manuscript for a sixty-poem collection, *Midwest Medley—Places & People, Wild Things & Weather.* I submitted the manuscript, along with a reading fee, to Kelsay Books and the manuscript was accepted for publication. I received five free books, a listing in the publisher's catalog, an Amazon listing, a copyright and an author's discount on future orders. The book received an *Outstanding Achievement in Poetry Award* from the Wisconsin Library Association in 2018.

Defining Success

Conventional wisdom can convey the impression that "coming close" in a competition means nothing. The opposite sentiment, found in vanity publishing, where, for a price, all participants get published, isn't much better. It's supposed to make you feel good but might just mean that you've spent thousands of dollars to find out that some poor-quality stuff is as good as yours.

However, a nomination for an award, being short-listed, a contest finalist or semi-finalist, are all measures of success. Accepting these designations as recognition of superior work, as they truly are, should help dispel some rejection anxiety. Coming close gets little respect in most activities. It's regarded as *a miss* rather than *a near win,* as it should be called. Success needs a better definition, a more encompassing one. Competition is fierce and to come close means something. It can be a step toward future, greater rewards.

Enjoy the contenders presented here and know that the hackneyed clichés still hold true: Persistence is the name of the game. It's never too late to start something new.

PART I

Going Places:
Here, There & Everywhere

A sidewalk café in Germany, charnel grounds of Tibet,
an imaginary voyage,
a poetic tour begins by questioning
the value of physical travel

Counting Cats

"Travel's a fool's paradise," so said Ralph Waldo Emerson:
A fool thinks he'll alter his life with a trip to Paris, Bangkok
or other exotic else, but finds, when opening his luggage,
he's still brought along himself.

A warning to trekkers about far-off travel, comes from
Henry David Thoreau: *"It's not worth the while, to go
'round the world, to count cats in Zanzibar."*

Most meaningful journeys occur without ever leaving home—
no need to change the landscape, he said, better instead
—to change the soul.

This was the first poem I wrote when I began writing poetry in 2013. I always liked Thoreau's advice that soul-searching rather than "counting cats in Zanzibar" was the most valuable kind of travel and would think about it when in a foreign country. It was accepted and published in *Your Daily Poem* in 2014. Here are a few YDP readers' comments:

"Nicely expressed, yet, one can travel everywhere, in the pages of a book, before the fireplace."

"No matter where you go, dogs run barefoot. But travel can benefit one, I guess."

"I love this! I usually travel alone, But she is right: I open my suitcase and there I am, croissants notwithstanding!"

Seven years later, "Counting Cats" was also published in the *Wisconsin Fellowship of Poets 2021 Calendar*. The calendar's theme for that year was "Home."

Wayfarers

Three dozen doves rise in unison,
    a gray-feathered canopy
        winging toward a struggling sun,
            as red dusk saturates the sky.
Flightless, we wander—
    adrift in an earth-bound limbo,
        searching for direction
    —nomads roaming boulevards—
the act of travelling
    more important
        than the destination.

"Wayfarers" was inspired by a group of mourning doves that blanketed my yard. Their cooing reminded me of my father's love for birds. Homing pigeons, relatives of the mourning dove, were popular pets in the 1920s when my father was growing up. My grandfather wasn't much of an animal lover, a trait he passed on to his children—no cats, no dogs, birds were the only exception—they loved birds and had a dovecote attached to their garage.

School children of that era knew about the famous war hero called *Cher Ami* (Dear Friend), a homing pigeon owned by the U.S. Signal Corps. Despite severe wounds, Cher Ami delivered, under heavy fire, the message that saved 200 American soldiers in France during World War One.

The bird ultimately lost its leg, was fitted with a wooden one and received the *Croix de Guerre* from France and a silver medal from U.S. General Pershing. Every kid in those days wanted a Cher Ami—a brave little, one-legged bird.

"Wayfarers" was rejected by two literary journals, revised and rejected four more times for a grand total of six rejections. It ultimately became part of my chapbook on travel, *The Port Side of Shadows* (Finishing Line Press).

Three years later, in April 2017, *Woodland Pattern Book Center* chose "Wayfarers" plus two other poems, (also included in this book) "Lorca's Duende" and "Lyon Gastronomique" to be featured on their blog for National Poetry Month.

Woodland Pattern of Milwaukee, Wisconsin, is a nationally recognized book shop with 25,000 book titles of poetry, said to be the most comprehensive center of its kind in the U.S.A.

No Photosynthesis Occurs

I remember eating white asparagus
at a sidewalk café
in the shadow of Cologne Cathedral
on an amiable day in June.

This seasonal ivory treat,
topped with sun-colored hollandaise sauce,
tastes best in the company of friends,
with glasses of pale German wine.

Recipe:
To cultivate white asparagus,
bury the shoots in dirt as they grow,
allow no exposure to sunlight.

Use the same process to produce
sterile, non-permeable minds.

White asparagus, or *spargel*, is considered a spring delicacy, particularly in Germany where the season, *Spargelzeit*, lasts from April when the asparagus begins to emerge from the soil, to late June, the beginning of summer. *Spargel*, similar to its green cousin but bitter if exposed to sun, is grown under a covering of mounded dirt and cloth or plastic tarps. I was introduced to this delicacy by a friend while visiting in Germany during *Spargelzeit*, the inspiration for the poem.

"No Photosynthesis Occurs," was written in 2014 while I reflected on my travels and saw that white asparagus would make a great metaphor. The poem was rejected by six literary journals, finally published by *Plum Tree Tavern* in July 2015, republished that year in *The Inquisitive Eater* and in 2016, chosen for inclusion in the anthology, *Best of Plum Tree Tavern*.

The poem was published again in June of 2022 by *Your Daily Poem,* where readers commented:

"The sparseness of the poem has such a huge impact! Great ending to a beautiful poem."

"I have two asparagus spears that will grow into ferns. I hope young minds do the same."

"There is no ambiguity here as the words clarify the comparison."

"Perhaps this process is not good for growing minds, but the pale asparagus surely left an impression that I can taste today!"

"Well, just when I thought it wasn't such a great poem, in the third stanza, you threw me for a loop and changed my mind."

Lyon Gastronomique

*How do you govern a country that has
two-hundred and forty-six varieties of cheese?*
—Charles de Gaulle

I remember my days in Lyon—
classical ruins on the sheer hillside,
Renaissance routes from street to street,
kaleidoscope colors of the ancient silk trade,
    —and most of all—
farmer's markets filled with splendor.

Premium beef, poultry of Bresse,
twenty-two species of potato,
deep-lake fish from the French Alps district,
wine from vineyards terraced in Roman times,
    —and cheese, beautiful cheese—
in shades from cream to amber.

Camembert and brie, munster and chèvre,
blue-veined cheeses of the central district,
cheese produced by one lone farmer
from a single herd of cows
—all with names—
that roam freely in the mountains.

"Lyon Gastronomique" is a tribute to the French city of Lyon. Located at the confluence of the Rhone and Saone rivers, Lyon, underrated as a tourist site, hosts 2,000 years of history. Architecture includes a Roman Amphitheater along with medieval and Renaissance structures.

Traboules, covered passageways between buildings, are a unique feature of the Old City that recalls the time when Lyon was the heart of the silk trade. These passages protected bolts of silk from damage by the elements as they were being transported from workshops. Today they are often used as "short-cuts" from one street to another.

The poem, however, specifically addresses the restaurants and outdoor food markets that are responsible for Lyon's reputation as *"the world capital of gastronomy."* I have memories of long tables, covered with every type of cheese. Unforgettable are the restaurants that serve *bouillabaisse* (a fish stew), *escargot* (snails), *mante* (manta ray filets), and *quenelles des Lyon* (dumpling-like concoctions mixed with pureed pike).

The poem received rejections from three journals in 2015, was published by *Mused* in 2016 and in 2017, was included in my chapbook, *The Port Side of Shadows.*

Woodland Pattern Book Center in Milwaukee chose "Lyon Gastronomique" and two other of my poems to be featured on their book blog for National Poetry Month, April 2017. *Your Daily Poem* (YDP) published it in 2023.

Lorca's *Duende*

An eerie and baffling sadness
—a sadness that dwells in the spirit,
a hold that grips the throat,
emptiness that follows tears,
leaves lifeblood frozen.

The soul's suffering
—its acute awareness of death—
in a heightened state of emotion,
in a heightened state of expression,
holds both agony and splendor.

All that has dark sound
echoes through shadowed alleys,
accepts limitations of reason—
      a sorrow that brings raw pain,
rouses throbbing anguish.

Some will know its soulfulness,
only when they are old, as I am—
the twisting knife of reality,
the frayed sound of nightfall.

Spanish poet and playwright, Federico García Lorca (1898–1936), murdered by Nationalist forces during the Spanish Civil War, coined the term *duende* ("ghost" or "goblin" in Spanish).

It is a concept that represents a dark and elusive force through which artists channel their creative power—moments in artistic activity when something else seems to take over, when something speaks through the artist. It is often associated with *flamenco*.

Seven literary journals rejected "Lorca's Duende" before *Silver Blade Magazine,* a journal for speculative and fantasy writing, accepted it.

Woodland Pattern Book Center chose it and two other of my poems to be featured on their book blog for National Poetry Month, April 2017. It was published in the chapbook, *The Port Side of Shadows* (Finishing Line Press).

Sketches Along the Yangtze

I. Solitude

Nothing but the moon attends ten thousand peaks along
the river. Forlorn wanderers in the gorges weep for home
when the gibbon's cry echoes. Only in this place can a traveler
hear sound so mournful.

II. Myth

The gorges run deep and long, sunlight rarely penetrates
green-clad pinnacles shrouded in a curtain of rain.
Here, an Immortal loved a mortal king, invaded his dreams
as a cloud at dawn and rain at sunset. Clouds and rain have
since begotten a symphony of longing.

III. Renewal

Ahead are the twelve peaks of Wu Gorge, a bleak and frothy,
dark place. The aura heavy, somber, desolate—waves churn,
roar, rush to the sky. Over the frontier pass, wind and clouds sink
to the waiting earth where million-year ancestries
embrace ancient terrain.

The mighty Yangtze crashes, carves its way to the sea.

A three-day trip on the Yangtze River in China inspired "Sketches Along the Yangtze," written in 2013 when I first began to write poetry.

The melancholy cry of the gibbon heard in the Yangtze River gorges symbolizes the sadness of travelers far from home. The phrase "clouds and rain" is a traditional Chinese euphemistic expression believed to have originated in myths about *Goddess Peak* along the Yangtze River. It alludes to having sex. Sexual references were barred in China, so the Chinese worked around the restrictions by inventing indirect language to talk about it.

Six journals declined the poem. One editor commented, *"in particular we enjoyed Sketches Along the Yangtze. Please feel free to submit again."* A second editor wrote: *"we enjoyed your poems, particularly 'Sketches Along the Yangtze,' however, we are going to pass on inclusion. We very much look forward to reading more from you in the future."*

I eventually learned to do a better job of matching poem styles to publication venues. These editors were telling me that my work was good, just not suited to their current publication.

Lost Tower Publications in the UK accepted "Sketches" for their anthology, *Journeys Along the Silk Road* in 2015. It featured writing inspired by China's ancient trade routes. "Sketches" is also published in my 2017 chapbook, *The Port Side of Shadows* (Finishing Line Press).

Ethereal Collision

Dies irae, dies illa . . . dona eis requiem*
   —13th Century Mass for the Dead

I: I'll tell you a tale of Hallowmas time, a triduum marking the Days of the Dead, three days of petition for the faithful departed, a time when the liminal veil linking material realm to the hereafter, thins—perilous dates when worlds clash under skies colored like ash from cremains, when trees moan and hedge-borders whisper, when believers pray loudly while walking near woodlands, to calm their fears, soothe the souls of the dead—when night ravens, messengers of Odin, call to the shades of worthy men, in a world where reason and myth collide.

II: A crew sailed from home one September, a month before Hallowmas time. Lost in yawning fjords where snow clouds converge, they steered hot-tempered seas with ruinous currents, faced vicious gusts that drove down from the foothills, screaming like squalls on a Patagonian plain. On the Eve of All Hallows, last day of October—first day of the Hallowmas trine—they entered emptiness soaked in shadow, pierced stillness on satiny water, continued adrift on November the first, Feast of All Saints—second Hallowmas day—crossing boundaries, almost unnoticed.

III: On the Day of All Souls, November the second—third day of the Hallowmas trine—a day of purple for those departed but not yet free of sin, booming movement spanned the sky at home port. Wolves howled, and woeful moans sounded, bells tolled for the restless dead. The ship's logbook surfaced in the waters of home port, last entry had four words recorded that motionless morning—*the veil is lifted*—sole trace of them ever uncovered, the end of their odyssey untold, a story in memoriam, met through the murmurs of ravens.

* *Day of wrath . . . Grant them rest.*

This fantasy is based on a *triduum,* literally meaning a series of three days. The term is used primarily to indicate the three-day Roman Catholic observance preceding Easter.

Hallowmas, used here, indicates an observance of the three-day season comprised of the *Eve of All Hallows* or Halloween (October 31), *All Saints' Day* (November 1, a feast day in honor of the saints and martyrs of the church), and *All Souls' Day* or *the Day of the Dead* (November 2), a time to remember those departed.

Hints from a poetry coach:

"This has a strong opening stanza, mysterious imagery, archaic language that evokes an older time . . . Of fisherman? or Sailors bound for England? I think if you specify, they will be clearly humans not ghosts on this voyage." (I didn't take the advice.) *"Can you provide a translation of the epigraph? I like this poem, just think it needs editing to make it stronger."*

I submitted this in 2014 to five journals that specialize in fantasy and horror. It was rejected by five journals. On my sixth try, in 2015, the journal, *Liquid Imagination—where reality and fantasy blur,* accepted it. Maybe the poem would have been better had I taken the coach's advice, but I felt the reader should decide if the men were human or ghosts. I did, however, add a translation of the epigraph to the end of the poem.

Impermanence

I've watched them soar at home
and in far-off places.
They tilt side to side as they float,

trace lazy rounds on the skin of the sky—
silent sailboats, six feet across,
catch a ride on thermal currents.

I once saw them from the top of a temple
circling charnel grounds in Tibet—
not messengers of bereavement,
but a sacred crew that attends the dead.

Dressed in mourning,
they glide elegantly on warm drafts.

When I see them soundlessly soaring,
I think of sky burials—
spirits riding on columns of air.

Open-air sites, or charnel grounds, are sacred areas in Tibet where the dead are left exposed to waiting vultures. This ancient practice is called *sky burial*. Various forms of excarnation (de-fleshing) have been practiced for thousands of years by cultures throughout the world. Tibetan Buddhists see earthly life as insignificant and impermanent. Sky burial is a last gift to the universe—a way to provide food for other living beings.

Sky burials originated as a pragmatic solution. The soil layer in Tibet is only a few inches deep, with permafrost underlying the surface, too hard and rocky to dig a grave. Most of Tibet is above the tree line. Due to the scarcity of timber, fuel for cremation is limited and economically unfeasible.

Only the family is allowed to attend the actual ceremony but as in the poem, I was on the roof of a nearby temple, able to see the birds circling. Many people find vultures loathsome and the subject of sky burial too disturbing. But in Tibet it is seen as a pious practice, where spirits glide in the air, freed of their bodies, providing life-sustaining nourishment to other creatures.

"Impermanence" was rejected seven times before finally being published in my chapbook, *The Port Side of Shadows* (Finishing Line Press). The writing coach I had at the time didn't like the poem, and obviously seven journal editors didn't either. Some find the subject too unsettling.

Thoughts of Alfred's World

A common enough sight across the moors
—disturbing when the wings move to town.
        —Alfred Hitchcock's "The Birds"

I saw starlings gather at Coventry in the West Midlands of England. Ebony feathers navigate moorlands, iridescent motion generates shapes in synchronized activity.

Moving as one in pulsating antics, they formed hourglass and funnel and ribbon designs, midair—an avian dance, dizzy in the evening sky, a murmuring* bird ballet.

A thousand wings moved to city treetops, some withdrew, more arrived on the scene—autumn-bared boughs drooped, weighed down with black feather foliage.

Unsettled, I shifted to shelter, turned locks, covered windows, hid from the cinematic sight as an encore formed in the distance. I saw starlings gather at Coventry in the West Midlands of England

—no one knows why they murmur.

---

* *Starling flocks "murmur" or fly in tight, swooping and fluid formations called murmurations.*

The inspiration for this poem came from an incident in Coventry, England. Hundreds of starlings filled the trees around my hotel *"with black feather foliage"* and I was immediately reminded of Alfred Hitchcock's horror film, "The Birds."

My poetry coach commented, "Good metaphors, here and throughout. I like your descriptions of their dance. I like your repeating the first stanza here—but do they really murmur? Can you briefly describe that sound in a line following this one?"

The references to "Alfred's world" in the title and the "cinematic" sight were understood as a reference to the Hitchcock film, but the word "murmuring" in this context, does not refer to a sound the birds make, although the sound of their wings is often called a *murmur*. It actually refers to the complex flight patterns they form. Starling flocks of five-hundred birds per flock, fly in dense, dance-like patterns, called *murmurations,* thought to possibly be for protection from predators.

Six editorial readers rejected the poem and may have been unfamiliar with "murmuring." I added an epigram and a footnote. The poem was published in my chapbook, *The Port Side of Shadows* (Finishing Line Press).

Traveling

He wanted to give me the whole world, he said, when we had dinner one June in Oakland. He scrambled up rocks in Alberta to prove it, collected wild goat hair for me to weave.

We walked amid sea elephants on a Pacific beach; didn't know how dangerous that was. He climbed the tower in Paris in August; nearly passed out and can't speak French.

He flew to Dresden and drove south to meet me; slept in a farm field along the way. He found me in Prague, unsure where I was staying, not even how he got there that day.

He missed a turn in a Sumatran jungle. I wasn't worried; he finds his way in odd places same as in a hometown grocery store. I arrived back at camp, and there he sat—drinking a cold one with monkeys.

We were drenched in drizzly Scotland; ate haggis and neeps washed down with brown ale. We drove thru bleached Spanish hill towns, explored a brocaded cave, then parted with tears at Malaga.

I shopped *souks* in Morocco, drank tea in a nomad's tent; but traveling's best with someone you love. He hunted oryx and kudu in Namibia; I'm not sure he noticed I wasn't there.

Seven journals rejected "Traveling," one of my first-year poetry efforts in 2013, though one editor did send encouraging words:

"We enjoyed the voice in your poems; in particular, we enjoyed 'Traveling.' However, it is not what we are seeking. We very much look forward to reading more from you in the future and encourage you to try us again."

After repeated tune-ups and seven rejections, I submitted "Traveling" to *Third Wednesday, A Quarterly Journal,* where it was accepted and published in 2014.

In 2019, when the collection, *Midwest Medley* (Kelsay Books) was honored by the Wisconsin Library Association, *Third Wednesday* republished the poem with my photo. They included congratulations on the award and announced that *Third Wednesday* was pleased to have first published "Traveling," a poem from the award-winning book.

It was at this point that I started to feel I was actually "a poet, writing poetry," not just "someone who writes poems."

Essaouira*

I receive impulses from the world—
> eavesdrop on the workings of this existence,
> explore the port side of shadows—
>> along my way to Essaouira.

The velvet dark embraces trepidation,
> foreboding I cannot explain—
> silent witness to changing seasons
>> —a reflection of the unknown.

I hear trees grow—
> they twist and bend across the gritty distance,
> wait in this place of imagination,
>> this place of ultraviolet light—and I pause.

I chase ghosts through the night, tread softly,

> listen closely as I walk—
> remember gulls that swoop
>> the beach, white goats in argan trees,
>> in this place that's called Essaouira.

---

*Essaouira *is a Moroccan city, pronounced* ess-we-rah

The line, "white goats in argan trees" often puzzles readers. Essaouira, an Atlantic port city in Morocco, is a center for argan oil production, one of the most expensive oils in the world. Goats climb the trees, feed on the nuts which pass whole through the goat's digestive system. The nuts are gathered from the goat droppings. Oil-bearing seeds, used in luxury cosmetics and for culinary purposes, are extracted from the nuts. Argan trees and tree-climbing goats are found only in Morocco.

I had been writing for about a year and a half when I started submitting "Essaouira" to literary journals. Five journals rejected the original version.

I took the advice of a poetry coach and made some changes:

"This is the most complicated poem in this packet of your poems . . . I love 'explore the port side of shadows'—that is gorgeous (and possibly a good book title. Hang onto it). Also, I hear trees grow / they twist and bend across the gritty distance—that stanza is quite good."

"The velvet dark stanza is less interesting as it is currently written: It 'tells' us statements rather than 'showing' us," (the most famous rule given to new poets—"show don't tell") *"and there is a lot of grand abstraction. On rewriting, trust the 'port side of shadows' . . . find those specific physical moments and words that will put us in that place."*

After the changes, three more journals rejected "Essaouira," a total of eight rejections. I included it in the manuscript for my chapbook in 2017 and used the coach's suggestion for the book's title, *The Port Side of Shadows*. One of these days I may rewrite it again.

The Saints Said Nothing

Thirty sacred statues—weathered stone and windswept metal—
border the Charles Bridge along the path to Prague Castle.
Travelers throng the crossway under the gaze of soundless saints.

Churches and chapels abound in wood-carved sanctity and relic
 bones. The Holy Infant in brocaded silk, jewel-laden madonnas,
avenging archangels in armor, look down from ornate altars
—painted mouths, frescoed faces—keep tomb-like silence.

Wenceslas the good king, saintly equestrian, shield of the lowly,
quietly presides over New Town Square.

The Apostle Clock in Old Town continues its medieval routine.
Twelve robotic disciples parade in mechanical order,
raise automated hands to bless crowds gathered below
as Death strikes the hour

—as empty eyes of clerics and lawmakers
watched trains depart for Terezin.*

* *Czech name for* Theresienstadt Concentration Camp, *northwest of Prague.*

The "Saints" was rejected four times before being published as part of the manuscript for the chapbook on travel, *The Portside of Shadows* (Finishing Line Press, 2017). It is a study in contrasts: the beautiful monuments of the city of Prague with the horrors of the World War ll Nazi occupation, as the famed Apostle Clock continues its medieval routine.

Established as a "model" camp to conceal the Holocaust from outside inspection, Theresienstadt or Terezin (Czech name), near Prague, served as a waystation to the death camps of Auschwitz and Treblinka.

To dispel rumors about the existence of extermination camps, the Nazis permitted the Red Cross to visit Terezin, but first arranged an elaborate hoax. They deported many camp residents to Auschwitz to minimize the appearance of overcrowding and erected fake stores and cafés to give it a "real life" appearance. They also performed a children's opera for the guests.

The hoax was so successful that the Nazis made a propaganda film about Theresienstadt showing how well the Jews were living under Third Reich protection. When the film was finished, most of the cast where deported to Auschwitz where they were executed.

Dancing *Flamenco* in Ronda

I went to Andalusia to breathe the spirit,
to feel the aura of Spanish hill towns.

In Ronda, a sky island perched on sheer cliffs,
spanning a canyon,
I found *flamenco* in a smoky *taverna*—
a singer's scorched voice,
the passion of a guitar
thick with soul-wrenching sorrow,
a dancer whose prime had passed—

unaware of anything around her,
she danced the rhythm of her beating heart,

danced as if life depended on dancing—
as if death might come any moment.

"Dancing *Flamenco* in Ronda" was inspired by a visit to cliff-nestled Ronda, a town divided by a deep rocky chasm, birthplace of bull fighting and home of the oldest bullring in Spain. It is one of Spain's oldest of the famed "White Towns of Andalusia," a place where locals still danced authentic *flamenco*.

Andalucía, an Islamic kingdom between the 8th and 15th centuries, was separated from northern Spain which was ruled by Christian kings. During this period of division, the use of lime to whitewash entire villages is said to have helped create a sense of unity between the Moorish pueblos of Andalucía.

Novelist Ernest Hemingway and actor Orson Wells were famous Americans who spent much time in Ronda. Both wrote of Ronda's bullfighting traditions and the scenic beauty of the area. The setting of Hemingway's novel, "For Whom the Bell Tolls" is believed to have been inspired by Ronda. Per his instructions, Orson Wells' ashes were buried in Ronda, the place where he felt most at home, rather than in his birthplace of Kenosha, Wisconsin.

In this poem, the dancer is filled with *duende,* and *"danced as if life depended on dancing."* The spirit of *flamenco,* called *duende,* is explained in my companion poem, "Lorca's *Duende,*" also found in this book.

Rejected by seven literary journals, "Dancing Flamenco" was published in my chapbook on travel, *The Port Side of Shadows* (Finishing Line Press, 2017) and by *Lucidity,* also in 2017. I recall that trip to Spain with much pleasure. Maybe nostalgia clouded my judgement, since seven editors didn't seem to appreciate the poem.

Expatriate

*Serenely let us move to distant places and let
no sentiments of home detain us . . . prepare
for parting and leave-taking or else
remain the slave of permanence*
—Hermann Hess

Rows of brick bungalows and two-flats,
an occasional white cottage, the corner store,
all in city-block order—
narrow back-alleys,
streets lined with spring-flowered catalpa trees,
their blossom clusters like cymbidium orchids,
their leaves, heart-shaped—
mothers in tidy houses sweep front walkways,
yet fallen red mulberries
still stain children's shoes—

what we have left, those who have left us,
images of long-past selves—
we carry them all, scattered through life
like last year's snow.

I wrote "Expatriate" about the neighborhood of my early childhood in Cicero, Illinois. I can still picture the street I lived on, the friends I had, the places we played. My parents bought a new house and we moved to another town when I was in seventh grade, age twelve.

I thought of "growing up and leaving" the neighborhood as a "migration" of sorts and submitted the poem for consideration in an anthology with the theme of "migration." The poem was not accepted for the anthology.

It was also rejected by four other literary journals and ultimately included in the 2017 chapbook, *The Port Side of Shadows—Poems of Travel*. "Expatriate" was later included in two literary publications, *Lucidity* and *The Museletter*.

PART II

Of Things Social:
Principles & Opinions

Sociological and political subjects join
gender equality
and bureaucratic paperwork

There Goes the Neighborhood

There are reports of *yetis*
in my neighborhood.

What will I do if hirsute humanoids
come lumbering through the yard?
Will my valiant guard cat snarl and hiss
or merely cry and hide?

Can they shatter glass,
reduce me to a jellied mass, a common lump,
depress the value of my house?
Should I ferret-out the twelve gauge?
—they have criminal leanings, you know—
or could it be a wiser choice
to unbolt the door and call,

"Care to join me for a cup of coffee?"

I liked the poem, "There Goes the Neighborhood" from the time it was still in the embryotic stage of development and thought the final product would easily be accepted by a journal on the first try. No such luck. It didn't find favor with any of the four journals to which I sent it.

Perhaps they didn't understand the metaphor? or they understood it too well? I sent it to places that ordinarily published socially relevant material, so it did go to what could be called "appropriate" places. I was forced to conclude that it might just not be a good poem, but I did include it in my *Midwest Medley* manuscript (Kelsay Books, 2018).

Jerry Apps, nationally known, award-winning Wisconsin author of rural history wrote a back-cover "blurb" for *Midwest Medley,* citing his five favorite poems from it, which included this poem. He wrote:

"I especially like . . . the great story, vast application and wonderful ending in 'There Goes the Neighborhood.'"

I respect Jerry and so I conclude that the editors missed a good poem. In the end, it all comes down to "taste."

Remembering Emmet Till

Let me peer out at the world through your lens . . .
Let me see how your blue is my turquoise
and my orange is your gold.
                              —Naomi Shihab Nye

Decades drift by—life a crowded stream.
Memories, like ripples, dissipate—
sights and sounds, smells and touch, deleted
so not to overwhelm with too much recollection.

We age—revisit erased images.
I see meaning now, in fields of cotton—
bolls nestled in dried bracts, sharp as razor blades,
harvested by bare fingers.

The air heavy with restraint, as silent men,
hats in hand, followed local protocol,
stood off in roadside ditches
until our car passed by.

This girl from somewhere in the North
—intrigued by a world she didn't know—
tried to socialize with those
expected to keep their distance.

I recall the look on Big Sam's face
when I showed up behind the main house
—alone—
where he was cooking catfish in an iron kettle
and I, unknowing, broke the silent code,
asked him friendly questions.

Now I know that look was fear.

"Remembering Emmet Till" was inspired by a true incident, where, as a teen-age girl from the Chicago area visiting in the South, I naïvely violated the code of behavior for a white female interacting with a black male. When I found the quote by Naomi Shihab Nye I knew it would be the perfect epigraph for a poem about my long-past visit.

Sam was hired to cook catfish for a welcome party. I had never seen anything cooked in a big iron kettle, over an open fire. I was curious, slipped out to the back of the house, alone, and went to where he was cooking. Sam, I thought, was acting strange. I was being friendly but he ignored me, never making eye-contact.

It was many years later that, reflecting on the era and the incident, I realized Sam was not being rude: he was afraid, not just fearful, but probably terrified. The case of Emmet Till was not too far in the past at the time of my visit. Emmet and I were similar in our ignorance. His mother warned him, but no one told me.

The 1955 case became a catalyst in the national Civil Rights movement. Emmet Till, a 14-year-old African-American boy from Chicago, was abducted, tortured and mutilated while visiting his relatives in the South. His mother had warned him that whites in the South could react violently to behavior that was tolerated in the North, but Till allegedly spoke too familiarly to a Mississippi white woman. His murderers were quickly acquitted.

The editor of one of the journals that did not accept the poem sent this note: *"Thank you for sending your work. We did admire it, and sincerely regret that we didn't find a spot for it in our upcoming issue. We wish you the best in placing this work and encourage you to submit to future issues."* After four journal rejections and one quarterfinals placing in a contest, *Mobius: The Journal of Social Change* accepted the poem in Fall 2021. It was also published in August 2022 by the journal, *Better Than Starbucks*.

Midterm Blossoms, 2018

With both attractive blossoms and sharp spines,
the night-blooming cereus rises amid restraint
and flowers during the night.

The night-blooming cereus
unfolds her petals on balmy evenings—
satin blossoms appear
from a dry, confining tangle.

Thorny stem, high-climbing,
the *Queen of the Night* ascends—
splendid scent grows as dusk deepens.

Her perfume rises, delights like a song,
majesty seen by the firmament's eyes—
beauty and spine most needed
when times are darkest.

"Midterm Blossoms, 2018," inspired by the midterm elections, was rejected by three journals before being published by *About Place Journal: Black Earth Institute,* a think tank dedicated to "reforging the links between art and spirit, earth and society."

My poem shares the same issue (Vol.5 Issue 3, May 2019) with notable poets, Joy Harjo, Rita Dove and others. Being in such excellent company feels as good as winning a prize—maybe better.

The poem uses the highly fragrant *night-blooming cereus,* a stunning cactus species, which struggles to grow and bloom under unfavorable conditions. It metaphorically speaks about the determination and ultimate success of female candidates in the 2018 midterm elections.

I Deal with "The Problem"

I dismiss guidance in self-help books on how to make life better, don't engage in feel-good activities either—perfumed candles, drinking Lady Grey tea—don't read trite quips on my Facebook page or indulge in chocolate bonbons and bubble baths.

Clear clutter from the closets, I say—nostalgia doesn't solve problems or make life better. Why save a dried-up prom corsage— watering it with tears won't revive a "Sweet Sixteen" romance.

Multi-taskers, nose-wipers, ladies-NOT-waiting—unsung heroines, Wonder Women, all—we'll be outrageous, take over the world, incite riots. It's time for upheaval. I'll get a tattoo, write a steamy novel, run for office, go back to school at age forty-two.

Even though the 19th Amendment happened over a hundred years ago, a gender gap still exists—equality's an uphill battle. It's past the hour. Past time to move on. There are other places to go.

Better Than Starbucks Journal accepted "I Deal with The Problem" in August 2021 after five literary journals rejected this call to arms that deals with self-help books, female stereotyping, and the gender gap. It's rather flippant but with a serious message.

(I confess: the poem isn't an accurate autobiography, although I did find the inspiration when I was cleaning a closet.)

Parts of the poem do hint at some things that parallel my life, but I'm not planning to get a tattoo; my dried-up prom corsages were thrown away a long time ago and I think I'll stick to writing poems not novels, but . . . my childhood friends and I often roll-played *Wonder Woman and Her Amazon Helpers*

. . . guess who I was.

Life in a Word

Stage I: Look at the word, *lust,* take an unvarnished view: craving, desire, an inordinate appetite, burning fire, a yearning for more than is required, an itch that needs persistent scratching. To lust after, to covet, to want, predisposes one to others of the Deadly Seven, like envy, greed, and gluttony. Lusty sex sins, attributed to mental disorder or concern unbuckled, committed by Hollywood types and alike by pious clerics sniffing perfume mixed with the scent of baby powder, generate psychological thoughts: how magnetic draw fades quickly—how sex without love just makes you sad.

Stage II: A word that defines a form of decay, *rust,* freezes motion, emotion, is a scale formed from disuse, a condition of oxidation, limitation: observe the person whose pinnacle occurred at age eight on the stage of *The Original Amateur Hour*. Rusted-shut is rigidity, inflexible and barren, neglect over time, a bureaucratic universe with cliché-filled dialogue, wordplay, and nonsense, byzantine utterances from pale-faced scholars. Find rust in cast-off devices, disintegration, waste from civilized living, corruption, tarnish, decomposition, politicians rusted in place, producing parodies of democracy.

Stage III: When examining *dust,* a word implying powder, dirt, earth, grime, think Dust Bowl with choking billows of dust that muddied the sky, black with soil turned to dust. Think loess: pale yellow, buff-color, dusty soil cover, fine particles, ground and pulverized, silt-sized sediment deposited by wind-blown dust. Dust-replacing-the-sea speaks of upheaval, great change, the passage of time, see the dusty world in a grain of sand. Ash, dusty residue, recap cremains, ashes-to-ashes, dust-to-dust, all that remains. Blow away, fade away, dissolve, dissipate, scatter—dry and bitter dust.

Commentary from a poetry coach: *"Wow! This poem really takes a lot of risks in jumping from image to image in a free form flow of language that is playful and at the same time completely loaded. Nice job! I like the three stages described and how they relate to each other."*

Some poems are a struggle to write. This was, for me, just the opposite—one of those poems that seemed to write itself, to take over, a rollercoaster ride that just goes!! When that happens, I am surprised and not always sure of where it came from (if you have read the earlier entries in this book, the phenomenon I'm describing is related to the concept of *duende,* found in the poem, "Lorca's Duende" in Part I.

There were unusual factors contributing to the inspiration behind this poem. I was preparing a calorie-laden dinner party and called the menu "A Seven Deadly Sins Dinner." From there, the poem developed. Rhyme stepped in and the words just kept on rolling and rolling . . . lust turned into rust . . . which turned into dust. The rest is history.

"Life in a Word" has an interesting publication past beginning in 2013. It was unsuccessfully entered in two contests and rejected by five literary journals. Ultimately accepted by *Camel Saloon* poetry journal, it was nominated for a *Best of the Net* literary award in 2014. Further, it was included in the *Best of Camel Saloon* anthology, rejected as a reprint in another journal, then published in the *Midwest Medley* collection (Kelsay Books).

I Listen to Gorecki's Symphony*

I hear a symphony of history's calamities—"one death a tragedy,
millions, a statistic." Grieve the small girl in a bright red coat—
days of sorrow—a landscape littered with ashes and bone.

A mother mourns her son, "Is he in a grave somewhere?—who'll
return him to me? Maybe he's buried in an unknown trench,
a ditch—filled with ashes and bone."

Her grieving recedes. She raises her head without despair—
"Songbirds sing to him, mild breezes blow, grass grows over him,
he sleeps peacefully"—courage born in ashes and bone.

Tendrils rise from cities of burnt-over rubble, from the mourning
of mothers. But fresh green springs through wreckage, through
sorrow—the nightingale still sings—amid ashes and bone.

Henryk Gorecki's Symphony No. 3 "Sorrowful Songs."

This poem was inspired by music, and the music that inspired it was inspired by poetry. I was listening to Henryk Gorecki's *Symphony No. 3* on Public Radio, swept up in the music's repetitive patterns. A soprano solo is featured in each of the three movements. Gorecki called it *Symphony of Sorrowful Songs*. The 1991 recording that features soloist Dawn Upshaw sold a world-record million-plus copies, unusual for a classical album.

Gorecki heard a 1920 Polish song about war that had, he said: *"a wonderfully poetic text. I do not know if a 'professional' poet would create such a powerful entity out of such terse, simple words. It is not sorrow, despair or resignation, or the wringing of hands: it is just the great grief and lamenting of a mother who has lost her son."*

Gorecki denied his symphony was about war, but he was further inspired by the inscription *"Oh Mamma do not cry"* scrawled on the wall of a Gestapo prison cell in occupied Poland.

Current world news had been reporting not only the wartime horrors of the people in Ukraine, but also their undaunted spirit and courage. The poem came naturally from the situation, with the repetition of the phrase, "ashes and bone" echoing the repetitive patterns of the music.

"I Listen to Gorecki's Symphony" was written and rewritten several times in 2022, submitted to *Verse-Virtual* in June and accepted the next day. I received a note from one of the contributing editors after the poem was published in July:

"Thank you for the synchronicity in your poem of music and image. I read your poem several times. What a wonderful construct of imagery."

Sometimes it happens that way. Not often . . . but sometimes.

Praise Paper and Red Tape

Your documents or your life
—Bill Kirby: *Fear, Fun and Filoz*

Praise birth certificates, deeds to buildings and land,
passport papers that permit travel, laminated paper that
bestows driving rights—praise essential papers.

Praise vaccination papers that say we, and the cat, are
safe to be around—you never need to worry if one of us
bites you—life's filled with red tape and essential papers.

Praise diplomas, papers that show we read all the books,
passed all the courses—and they don't tell if we learned
anything elemental, so—praise essential papers.

Praise the papers that seal a marital agreement, a promise
on paper, to stay wedded together until one of the pair is dead
—or has been unfaithful—which generates more essential paper.

If your birth records can't be found, and there's no official
certificate, it must mean that you've never been born, and so
—will never die. Praise red tape.

Bill Kirby writes a blog called *Fear, Fun and Filoz*. "Praise Paper and Red Tape" was inspired by that column. The poem zipped along, seemed to write itself, and on the first attempt, was chosen for publication. *Highland Park Poetry* accepted it for the 2022 Summer Muses' Gallery and also for the anthology, *Odes: Poets Praising People, Places & Things*. It is one of those wonderful poetry stories, a fairy tale you hope will repeat, but seldom does:

You get an idea for a poem—in this case from a blog—the first draft goes pretty well. You subsequently do two re-writes, choose a publication, submit the third version to it. Three months after reading the blog, you are notified that your poem is going to be included in the Highland Park Poetry's online "Summer Muses' Gallery" AND will also be published in a print anthology on Odes. It doesn't get much better than that—only seventy-nine days from initial inspiration to publication and ah, yes . . . a double hit at that!!

But it does get better:
In November 2022, you are notified that Highland Park Poetry nominated your poem, "Praise Paper and Red Tape" *for a Pushcart Prize*. WOW!!!

Ever since I first heard about the *Pushcart Prize,* I had hopes of being nominated someday. I don't yet know the results for this year, but it's great to be nominated. Since 1976, the *Pushcart Prize* has honored the best writing (short stories, essays and poems) published in the previous year by small presses. Editors nominate up to six pieces that appeared in their publication. Of the approximately 10,000 nominations, 60–70 are awarded the prize each year and published in the *Pushcart Prize Anthology*.

Some say only a *win,* not just a *nomination,* is significant. I say that's "sour grapes," probably from authors who were never nominated. Does an *Emmy* or *Oscar* or *Pulitzer* nominee, who didn't win, not include the nomination as an accomplishment?

Feral Tenacity

I'm not a hothouse flower,
a rose with satin skin,
a blossom of waxy perfection,
here for merely a day.

I am a wildflower,
a perennial in an open field
that explodes
with perfumed abundance—
my essence
emerging like hidden fragrance.

I am a weed,
lithesome and supple,
sprouting free
in the cracks of a city sidewalk,
on the boundaries
of an uptown boulevard.

See me in the sunshine,
see me in the rain.
I'm not a hothouse flower,
and I'm no man's *boutonniere,*
and I'm not some shrinking violet
here for merely a day.

Women Speak, a painting and poetry collaboration hosted by the *Frank Gallery* of Chapel Hill, NC in 2018, featured artist Nancy Smith's water media and collage paintings of women. Poets were invited to submit a poem inspired by one of the paintings. Poems inspired by works of art are described as *ekphrastic.*

The chosen poems, printed, framed and hung in the gallery alongside the paintings that inspired them, would be published in a full-color catalog of the show. The poets were also to receive a *giclée* (zhee·klay) print of the original painting. My choice of a print to write about was a nude woman with flowing hair, titled "From the Depths of Earth."

I received notification that my poem was one of 22 selected from 327 entries: *"Congratulations! Thank you so much for submitting your beautiful piece, 'Feral Tenacity', to the Women Speak project. The panel of judges were delighted with your work!"*

The framed print hangs in my bathroom.

The poem was later rejected by a literary journal but accepted by *Your Daily Poem,* where it received comments from some appreciative readers:

"Charming and amusing last verse" . . . *"Brilliant!!"*

"Love this! Good job, Pat."

PART III

Nature:
trees, the sky, some fur & some feathers

A coverlet of snow, a blanket of darkness,
diamonds sparkling in the sky,
quiet evenings

The Breadcrumb Plate

Artic juncos, wintering here,
walk 'round it cautiously;
nuthatches, like chickadees
and cheeky jays,
dive in unceremoniously,
wing away with a prize.

The flicker's scarlet mark
holds brilliant against winter grays,
though humbled by
the allover glory of cardinals,
who elegantly ignore
the proffered plate.

"The Breadcrumb Plate" was accepted by *Peninsula Pulse* in 2013, the first year of my poetry journey. It was later rejected by another journal. The *Wisconsin Fellowship of Poets* included it in the *Fall Conference Program, 2016,* and in 2018 it was published in the collection *Midwest Medley: Places & People, Wild Things & Weather* (Kelsay Books).

When I was assembling it, my coach thought "The Breadcrumb Plate" was a good poem to use for the book's title. She wrote:

"Wonderful! Maybe this is your title poem?"

But I didn't feel it was strong enough to be the book's title. I was set on using a photo of my battered mailbox for the cover with the word "Midwest" somewhere in the book's title.

(The poem behind that eventual title is "Futile Struggle: Salute to the Rural Mailbox," found here in Part 4.)

Villanelle for the Birch: An Arboreal Romance

Trees, it turns out, make all kinds of noises . . .
—Smithsonian Magazine

Birch trees have heartbeats, it's been discovered.
       Verdant boughs stir during waking hours.
Slumber entwined, arboreal lovers.

A mellow pulse, barely heard by others,
       purrs unruffled, whispers during showers.
Birch trees have heartbeats, it's been discovered.

Dusk descends—a tender, gentle mother—
       unfurls her cloak, enfolds leafy bowers.
Slumber entwined, arboreal lovers.

The canopy stirs, it lightly hovers,
       branches shift slowly with inner power.
Birch trees have heartbeats, science discovered.

Limbs slightly contract, then they recover,
       heart beats hum softly as morning flowers.
Slumber entwined, arboreal lovers.

Much is unknown, much left to uncover.
       Love, an enigma, baffles, empowers.
Birch trees have heartbeats, it's been discovered—
       slumber entwined—arboreal lovers.

National Geographic ran information about trees that I thought would be good subject matter for a *villanelle*. Trees, they said, *"make all kinds of noises as they grow and respond to their environment."* I wanted to try my hand at writing a *villanelle*, a complex, poetic form with a specific structure. If you check a writer's manual for a definition, this is what you'll find:

A French verse form consisting of five three-line stanzas and a final quatrain, with the first and third lines of the first stanza repeating alternately in the following stanzas. These two refrain lines form the final couplet in the quatrain. It uses repeated lines and a strict rhyming pattern throughout nineteen lines grouped into six stanzas.

My formal poem won third place in the *Kay Saunders Emerging Poet Competition, 2019,* sponsored by the *Wisconsin Fellowship of Poets*. Ironically, it has been rejected by eight literary journals. I sent it only to places that stated in the submission guidelines that they were open to all styles, including formal ones. Although a prize winner, it has never been published, thus, this book is its public debut.

I have written several types of formal poetry and admire Dylan Thomas's "Do Not Go Gentle Into That Good Night" (probably the best known villanelle, it is an argument that people should fight fiercely against death). I prefer *free verse* but writing complex rhyming forms is a challenge, a satisfying exercise in writing. Making lines rhyme is not difficult, but to make rhyming lines fit in a well done, formal structure, is a challenge.

The villanelle has been called the "most dreaded" poetic form, the most difficult to write well—"the poet's triple axel." After eight rejections, I guess "triple axels" are out of my league. I'd better stick to "figure eights."

Home Sweet Home Concerto

I
Forest interiors
shelter tree trunks split by lightening,
strangely shaped lifeless wood.
Lichen patches, like dermal abrasions,
creep and encrust ancient, grayed timber.
Deadly mushrooms in lurid hues,
threaten the unaware.

II
If you've never seen red sumac leaves
fierce with autumn,
then you've never seen vermillion.
Take a swig of the color,
sniff the scene, eye, don't finger—
lush crimson colonies
brocaded with jade and gold,
scaling tree shafts, disguising ditch slopes,
might just be venomous ivy.

III
Gnarled pines widen at root level—
sun drops down, rocks abandon the day's heat,
wind whirls overhead.
Frosted landscapes, fractured
like shattered glass, conjure a scrapbook
of the season's bullying chill—
snow brings a four-coat winter.

Coda
A place of harsh beauty like no other.

My first poetry coach commented on "Home Sweet Home Concerto," stating,

"I like the coda stanzas' imagery and precise 'seeing.' I'm not sure which place you're referring to here—perhaps clarify by putting a place name in the title?"

I didn't take the coach's advice on changing the title because I wanted "Home Sweet Home" to refer to a general place even though the poem has some regionally specific descriptions.

Readers can apply their own idea of *home,* since the poem implies that in spite of its drawbacks, *home* is still sweet. Titles are an important part of a poem and maybe I would have been more successful in getting it published if I had taken the coach's advice.

The *Avocet Weekly* published "Home Sweet Home Concerto" in August 2014 after seven journals rejected it. It is included in both the *Port Side of Shadows* and *Midwest Medley*.

Night Comes

> *Fate brings us all to the same place*
> —Appointment in Samarra

I walk the course
as night uncurls its fingers.

Dark elegance unfolds
before my eyes,
a stately door closing on the day.

Creature sounds squeeze my senses,
dark wolves intone a soulful note
as feathered sails swoop—

bring quick and silent passing.

Epigraphs are short quotes found at the beginning of a poem or other literary text, which belong to a different author. They work as a clue to the meaning of the poem or story that follows. O'Hara's words from his novel, "Appointment in Samarra" serve as an epigraph to this short poem, "Night Comes."

There is further meaning if the reader knows that John O'Hara, quoted here, also used an epigraph to the novel "Appointment in Samarra," His epigraph is the W. Somerset Maugham retelling of an ancient Mesopotamian tale:

A merchant in Bagdad sent his servant to the marketplace. When the servant returned, white and trembling, he told the merchant that in the marketplace, a woman he recognized as Death made a threatening gesture toward him. Borrowing a horse, he fled to Samarra, a distance of about seventy-five miles, where he believed Death would not find him.

The merchant then went to the marketplace, found Death, and asked why she made a hostile gesture to his servant. She replied, That was not threatening, it was only a gesture of surprise. I was astonished to see him in Baghdad, for I have an appointment with him tonight in Samarra.

This ancient tale, combined with creature sounds I've heard in the quiet night, served as inspiration for the poem. "Night Comes" was only declined once before *Poetry Quarterly* accepted it for publication in the Spring 2020 issue.

Magic in Collapsing Stars

> *Somewhere, something incredible*
> *is waiting to be known*
>   —Carl Sagan

We are made of the stuff of stars,
a taste of the wild, covered in forests
and meadows.

We are solitary nights, silent,
the quiet of space broken only by
the hoot of an owl.

We occupy a minute place, not lofty,
not specially charmed.
Stay—be here with me
    —just breathing.

A poetry coach who critiqued some of my early work, said of "Magic in Collapsing Stars," written in 2015 after two years of writing poetry:

"This poem is a giant YES for me. Love it. Beautiful. You should be sending this one out . . . in the very last line, I find that word 'stay' so poignant that I want to know who the speaker is talking to at that moment."

I was inspired to write this poem after reading some of Carl Sagan's quotes and submitted "Magic in Collapsing Stars" to seven journals. It was rejected seven times. My book, *Midwest Medley* (Kelsay Books), includes it.

Later published in *Lucidity,* it was also accepted for the *Wisconsin Department of Natural Resources 2020–2021 Calendar*.

Magic Evenings

We occupy a charmed place—
a patchwork of stars,
where solitary nights and silent space
are fractured by the hoot of an owl.

Stay, be here with me,
—just breathing.

The Waupaca, Wisconsin, Community Arts Board, dedicated to incorporating the arts into everyday life, sponsored a poetry contest as part of their *Main Street Redevelopment Project.*

Sixteen poems would be chosen to be imprinted in the new sidewalks along Main Street, creating the "Poetry at Your Feet" permanent display.

Poets, asked to capture the essence of the Waupaca area in their poetry, were challenged with the physical limitations of a concrete slab and a character count of under three hundred, including all characters, letters, spaces, and punctuation. Submissions from thirty-one cities brought in more than two hundred poems.

"Magic Evenings" written in 2021, is based on my previous poem "Magic in Collapsing Stars," streamlined to fit the requirements of a concrete sidewalk, was one of the final sixteen selected.

Midnight Encounter

Have you seen a badger up close—
that notoriously cantankerous carnivore.
Not unlike the looney cartoon,
he's America's answer to a Tasmanian devil.

Fierce, striped face, twenty pounds heavy
—about as big as my rather large cat—
flat and low-slung, wedge-shaped body,
steel-strong curved claws,
coarse grizzled coat, marked white and black.

One summer night I encountered this predator,
rooted in the middle of the road.
He stood in the headlights, refused to budge,
glared unswervingly, bared wicked teeth—
hissed a spine-chilling guttural growl,
snarled a dare.

Badgers attack things, I'd heard,
that far outweigh them, even an automobile.
Rather than risk a ruptured tire,
I smiled at his swagger and patiently waited
'til this undaunted spirit, this tough survivor,
decided to move on his way.

"Midnight Encounter," about a chance meeting with our local "Tasmanian devil," inspired this autobiographical poem. Rural Wisconsinites meet a lot of things along the road at night—deer, racoon, opossum—but I wasn't expecting a badger. They are abundant in Wisconsin but evasive, with a reputation for ferocity when encountered. The short, stocky, solitary and defiant animal has exceptionally long, thick, digging claws.

The poem was submitted to the *Poetry Quarterly Rebecca Lard* contest. It made the contender's list, did not win, but received Honorable Mention and was published in the Spring 2017 issue. Later published in *The Avocet*, a reader sent a note, stating,
"Glad you both survived the encounter!"

It was included in *Midwest Medley,* and *Your Daily Poem* accepted it for National Badger Day (October 3) where readers commented:

"Now I want a National Possum Day here in NC. They're not so fierce, but when they hiss, watch out!! . . . Love this badger poem!!"
. . . *"I've never spotted a badger in my neighborhood, but ever since one of them dug a hole beneath the utility company's 'No Digging' sign, I've suspected they have a good sense of humor."*

. . . *"I have had encounters with badgers in my native state of Colorado and even found them in the tundra, above timberline. Give them space, like you would a bear. This is a great tribute to a wonderful critter"* . . . *"this is truly a painting with words."*

Dubbed the "Badger State," the badger has long been part of Wisconsin's heritage. The University of Wisconsin adopted it as a mascot in 1889 and in 1957, the badger became the official state animal. The state's nickname, however, did not originate with the animal. Lead ore miners settled Wisconsin in the early1800s. They sheltered in the hillside mines or "holes" they dug looking for ore, "lived like badgers" because of harsh winters. Thus, local residents called the miners "badgers."

Some Things Die Before Called

Big box stores ran end-of-winter sales—
the groundhog predicted
spring was soon to come,
the calendar revealed
winter's conclusion—

but winter never ended,
spring never came.

April drizzle, not sweet and languid,
but sleety and raw
like February,
spat ice and snow—

winter never ended,
spring never came.

The globe is murky, the solar star frozen,
the lunar orb immobilized—
we long for something
not to be found—

You left in winter,
spring never came.

Gloomy weather that intruded into the time for spring and renewal, inspired this poem. The harsh, late winter weather was something that could easily and metaphorically be linked to or speak to, a personal loss of any kind. Could be of individual loss—a friend, a lover, a pet—or address other discouraging situations.

Unsuccessfully submitted five times (three contests and two rejections by journal editors) "Some Things Die" was eventually accepted by *Red Booth Review* with an enthusiastic note:

"We love 'Some Things' It's gorgeous"—

. . . certainly testament to the fact that one editor's taste isn't the ultimate judgement. Editors are human, have likes and dislikes. There are few rules in writing poetry.

"Some Things Die" was also included in the anthology, *Best of Red Booth Review* and finally, translated into Chinese and published in *Poetry Hall, Journal of the Chinese Poetry Association,* a bilingual publication. Guess I'd say that despite five "thumbs down" decisions, it was a success.

Wait 'til Tomorrow

Pines and oaks
weigh down
with winter burdens—
time's corroding tarnish
bonds
to souls and thoughts.

Sometimes it seems
the better course
to not stand up again—
but dawn ascends
and a fresh-born day
unwraps.

A writing coach thought there were too many abstractions in this poem but liked the last two lines—"and a fresh-born day unwraps"—could be a tactful way for her to say, "Not much here, but at least it has a positive closing."

It was 2013, early (the first year) in my poetry-writing venture. I entered "Wait 'til Tomorrow" in a contest where it earned no special recognition. I made some revisions and it was accepted and published by *Poetry Quarterly* whose editor commented:

I appreciate the symbolism . . . lovely tone here too, something transcendent going on, like wisdom recounted . . . nice poem.

His words encouraged me since busy editors don't usually give personal feedback and this did not have the sound of a form letter.

The poem is an upbeat response to the previous poem, "Some Things Die Before Called." They are effective when read as a pair.

Winter Sunlight

Though we're surrounded
by polar cold, the sun is on fire.

Slivers of silver
frost north-facing windows
in web-like patterns,
undisturbed by beams
that challenge fresh, white snow.

Rays wander in all directions,
play across a spectral landscape,
dance on buried grasslands,
frolic atop shrouded rooftops.

I wish you the eyes to enjoy it.

Winters in the frozen North may seem unending, but ice and snow can be inspirational. "Winter Sunlight" suggests that we live in a winter painting. My kitchen windows offer a vista of Nature's artwork, a reminder to enjoy the beautiful things that surround us rather than focus on the inconveniences winter sometimes brings.

Submitted to two journals, it was rejected by both. On the third attempt, it made the final round for the 2020 Rebecca Lard Award and was published in the Fall 2020 issue of *Poetry Quarterly*. Not a prize winner but being published and chosen for the finals was one of those "almost" wins I consider positive feedback.

The poem was subsequently accepted for publication in the *Wisconsin Department of Natural Resources 2023 Calendar*, ten years after it was first written.

Insomnia

You might sit up at night like Carl Sagan,
thinking about asterisms
or debris from a cosmic collision
spiraling toward the sun

—or imagine

how dust in the desert
or smoke in an airless room,
hangs suspended.

You might wonder,
when you stir from the depths of a dream,
if the noise you heard
was a thief on the stairs

—or the scratching of a mouse.

You might stay awake
and eavesdrop on conversations
between denizens of the dark
and the man in the moon

—or look up

and marvel at the ebony emptiness
of an unclouded country sky,
unmarred by light from a city.

"Insomnia" is one of my favorite nature poems. Written in 2016, it was entered in a contest, where it received no recognition, was submitted to and rejected by a journal, then published as part of the *Midwest Medley* manuscript in 2018. It was also published in *The Avocet* journal in December of 2020.

I've lived in the rural Midwest for most of my life, but still marvel at the "unclouded country sky." I have, however, noticed a change over the past forty years: the night sky is still ebony dark, peppered with silver stars, but now there is a narrow slice of soft light creeping up on the horizon that marks the expansion of a city thirty miles away. I fear the "ebony emptiness" is disappearing.

As of January 2022, there are 195 certified "International Dark Sky Parks" in the world, including the newest, *Newport State Park* on the tip of the Door Peninsula in Wisconsin. It was named to the *International Dark Sky Association*'s list of fantastic dark skies around the world. Newport is the first park in Wisconsin to receive the honor, joining the ranks of Big Ben, Glacier and Grand Canyon national parks.

Whiteout Report

Whiteouts arise
when snow falls dense and fast.
Wind gusts blind, push bodies off course,
cause confusion.

Inner bearings scrambled,
pathways indistinct,
can't tell sky from ground—

adrift in motion-filled curtains
impossible to penetrate—
lost a few feet from safety.

Whiteouts can happen
on summer days with minimal wind,
they come in many guises
—all dangerous.

"Whiteout Report" written in 2015, was rejected three times before being published that year in *Plum Tree Tavern,* an online journal, and included in the collection, *Midwest Medley* (Kelsay Books, 2018).

In my first two years of writing, I worked with several writing coaches, trying to make up for my lack of training in creative writing. This was one of the final poems I sent to my last coach. She didn't like the poem, particularly the last stanza, said all she knew was *"Whiteout is that thick chalky stuff we used to cover typewritten mistakes."*

It didn't occur to me that someone wouldn't know that the poem compared a blinding snowstorm, called a *whiteout,* to situations where people are "blinded" to something. The first stanza explains the term, or so I thought. But, if you live in the South, as the coach does, it is possible that you never have heard of a "whiteout," a condition where swirling snow severely reduces visibility and contrast, causing the horizon and physical features of the terrain to become obscured.

I remember "old timers" telling stories about their experiences with whiteouts. Perhaps the tales were embellished but it was dangerous to leave the safety of the house to go to the barn during a whiteout. There were reports of people losing their bearings, getting lost between the barn and the house and freezing to death. As a safety measure, they would keep a "lifeline"—tie one end of a rope to the house and the other end to the barn. Those animals had to be tended, no matter the weather.

The poem speaks to life's irony, draws attention to the wider issues in human nature and behavior. Yes, we need to know about all sorts of whiteouts.

In Praise of Challenging Cycles

Freed of ice, rivers murmur rippled melodies.
Butterflies, befuddled by plum-scent,
frenzied by desire, cartwheel in the breeze.
Gaunt pines survive challenges of time and weather
—old stalwarts, cloaked in new glitter,
tease with promise.

Rain and sunlight bathe kaleidoscopic blossoms,
bring splendid lushness—
scarlet scent anoints the air.
Tomatoes ripen on the vine, melons drip richness
—shapely potatoes mature without concern
for tests of early frost or future ice and snow.

Visitors gone—serene, almost noiseless
—only the rustle of painted foliage—
days of leisure, lavished with gold.
No wish to wear the skin of former times
or waste seconds in idle banter, no fear
of the bitter clasp to come, a minor-key lament.

Minimalism rules—a pared landscape, elegant,
crisp in black and white—little means,
utmost effects—limits of endurance tested.
 So much more than teasing promise, splendid
 lushness, lavish color—

less is more

Two literary journals rejected "In Praise of Challenging Cycles," written in 2017. One of the rejections included a note of explanation from the editor:

"In Praise of Cycles . . . received second-round consideration . . . our readers agreed the imagery is fantastic and the construction is skillful, (but) . . . the overwhelming majority of our submissions concerned nature and rural life thus we had to let many quality yet too similar poems, go . . . several hundred pieces were submitted."

Bramble, Journal of the Wisconsin Fellowship of Poets accepted "In Praise of Challenging Cycles" for publication in the Winter 2018 issue, which examined how poets think about meeting writing challenges, and how those challenges inform the words.

I felt that to write about subject matter as over-used as "the four seasons," the poem would be most effective if it ended with praise for winter's lack of the "flashiness" of color displayed in the other three seasons. That created the basis for a concluding line that used the seemingly contradictory, but favorite phrase of the modern architectural arts, "Less is More."

The poem was also entered in a contest where it received no recognition. It is included in the *Midwest Medley* collection (Kelsay Books, 2018) and appeared in the *Wisconsin Department of Natural Resources Calendar for 2020–2021*.

Elegy Before Snow Falls

Flowers grow out of dark moments
—Corita Kent

When autumn's equinox arrives,
and the flute's lament sails the wind,
place pleasing things
on the graves of the cherished dead.

When plums ripen to fragrant scarlet,
before winter's shroud wraps the fields,
roam the hills with the mournful task
of gathering fall's last flowers—
scatter them, with abundant tears,
on the graves of the cherished dead.

They live when those alive
remember them—Sleep sweetly.

Rejected by five journals, "Elegy," written in 2018, made the second round in a contest and the final round of *Midwest Review's* "Great Midwest Poetry Contest, 2019." Of course, I wish it had won, but it did come close.

The *Midwest* editor added:

"We appreciate the opportunity to consider your work . . . we received many strong submissions and though yours, among them, made it to the final round of consideration, I regret to say it was not among the ten finalists . . . hope to see more of your work."

Editors and coaches recommend that poets send work to editors who express interest in seeing more. They are not just being "nice," they really want to see it. I consider making it to the final round and receiving positive comments from editors a "win."

Through my own fault, this poem was erroneously coded as "published" in my files and thus I did not continue sending it out . . . so this is its first publication.

Night Music

Nightfall is the finest time to visit our country haven.
We escape to forest green that shrouds the eaves—
leave the clatter of a settled world.

I dream of unwinding there, nestled deep in a downy settee,
hearing a symphony of darkness—

web-footed songsters and untamed canines sing cantatas
under an effervescent sky.

We sip blush wine in the nippy breath of night
by light from a fire's flicker
and watch shadows slant across our reverie.

One of my earliest poems, "Night Music" was written in 2013. This take on country living was well-received by my first poetry coach, who commented:

"Very evocative! This poem sets a very sensual mood."

But in spite of her positive assessment, it was rejected by five literary journals over the next four years.

My first experience of actual country living, not just vacationing, was the initial inspiration for "Night Music." My permanent move to the wild countryside was gradual, but as I wrote, the total experience of moving from an urban setting to a completely rural one, blended. So many years have passed since the initial move that I have a problem imagining life somewhere else.

"Night Music" was ultimately published in both my chapbook, *The Portside of Shadows* (Finishing Line Press, 2017), and the collection, *Midwest Medley* (Kelsay Books, 2018).

PART IV

Humor: Not Only Light Verse, But Also Ironic, Satirical

Some serious art that's funny—some that's funny but not serious. Figure out which is which

Juvenal Knew About Suffering

I've been around enough years
to know about life on this plane—
many more years than needed,
to see misery as manifest fate.

Buddhists assert
that seeking contentment is fruitless.
They say life means cyclical struggle—
aiming to escape it is futile.

Juvenal knew the hazards of life—
knew all about suffering and pain.
Perils he cited were
fires, falling buildings
—and poets reciting in August.

"Juvenal Knew About Suffering," rejected only once before *Lake City Lights* accepted it, was written during 2013, my first year of submitting to journals. It takes a humorous and somewhat sarcastic approach, with poets the butt of the joke.

Juvenal, a Roman poet active in the late 1st to early 2nd century AD, became famous for his "savage wit and biting descriptions of life in Rome." His exaggerated, comedic work entitled "Satires" could be read as a critique of Rome. Using humor and ridicule to disparage society, he listed the ways in which Rome had become an "unbearable place to live," for which he was banished and his property confiscated.

Present-day examples of social satire are plentiful. They include the newspaper, *The Onion,* TV shows, *The Daily Show, Saturday Night Live* and others.

Land of the Lost: Unmatched Performance

I think he takes his socks off
all over the countryside.
Every week another one of a pair
disappears, unaccounted for,
gone AWOL or M.I.A.

I don't buy his "Missing Sock Theory"
—the wash-machine eats them up—
or the notion that hungry gremlins
slink into the hamper
and feast on its fetid tenants.

Haunted by the sobs
of their deserted sock mates
—with hope that some of the prodigals
will find their way home—
I keep adding the abandoned partners
to a rubber-banded bunch in his drawer.

So far, the bundle just gets bigger.

This poem appeared, almost spontaneously, when I was sorting the household laundry. It was born of frustration, a poem that developed quickly, a piece of "light verse" that carries a sting and doesn't need to be dissected to find the meaning.

Ultimately, its sprinkling of sarcasm about an everyday happening goes beyond my house—I suspect incidents like this cause exasperation and aggravation in many other households.

A poem just for fun, it was accepted in 2019 on the first try by *Your Daily Poem,* with some comments from readers:

"Yes, what DOES happen to those socks? I have many mateless ones! Love this poem!"

"Tell your husband that unmatched socks are now in style and begin making new pairs."

Carpe Diem—Seize the Day

I want to run away and be a Las Vegas showgirl—
glamour, fun, excitement—now that's an enticement.
What would my in-laws, the book club, the church-ladies say?
Carpe diem—seize the day.

I'd hire a maid, flee the cleaning, no more harsh detergent,
treat my skin with French-milled soap. Then there's
the kids—that's urgent—but let the chips fall as they may.
Carpe diem—seize the day.

There I'd be—wrapped in a white feather boa, nothing else.
My husband, stunned, the audience clamoring for more.
I'm a star, have fame galore, with rich admirers at bay.
Carpe diem—seize the day.

My bubble burst—glimpsed me in the mirror. All that's left
of my sweet reverie is a white feather floating in the breeze,
escaped the pillow when I made my bed. Guess a feather's
as close as I'll ever be—

hummmm . . . . . . maybe I'll dye my hair red.
Carpe diem—seize the day.

Unlike many of my poems, this narrative is not autobiographical although the message is something I believe: while some dreams seem unrealistic, "it's never too late to pursue something new" and "we lie in the bed we make."

Many traditional literary journals rarely publish humorous poetry unless it is metaphoric or employs irony. They state in their submission guidelines that all types of poetry are "considered" for publication but advise submitters to read the journal in order to see what types are "preferred." Not everyone finds humor, humorous.

I was unaware of the perils associated with submitting humorous poetry when I proposed this to *Lake City Lights* in 2013. It was the thirty-eighth poem I had ever written and the first one submitted to a literary journal. "Carpe Diem" was accepted. I was excited and unaware that this was not likely to happen again any time soon.

Five journals which accept previously published work, rejected it. In the years that followed, *ReVerse* and *Your Daily Poem,* geared to a general readership, accepted it three years after it was written and first published.

Positive comments from YDP readers included:

"Love the bubble-bursting stanza after all the build-up in the beginning!"

"I laughed aloud at the very first line!"

"Love this! The escaped feather is brilliant."

"Very unique and creative!"   *"Fun.!!! Wonderful!!"*

Five years after writing it, I included "Carpe Diem" in the *Midwest Medley* collection. I still manage a laugh and avoid the mirror.

Never Know What You'll See in Wisconsin

It was a dismal day when the peacock escaped.

A passerby spotted him strutting westward,
but a week-long fruitless search
dashed all hope of recovery.

I fear, they said, he came to a gruesome end,
converted to road-kill—
or the victim of famished critters—

could be coyotes or wolves—

or that peculiar neighbor
who'd shoot blue-plumed poultry
for a singular Sunday dinner.

But I like to think he is running free,
the thrill-seeking leader of a wild turkey gang—

metallic blue head, elegant crest,
the fantails of his flock-mates outclassed
by his shimmery train—

as he breeds upheaval
among flirtatious turkey hens.

A true incident was the inspiration for this piece. Our neighbors had a pair of peacocks. As reported in the poem, the male escaped and was never seen again.

Here in Central Wisconsin we have large flocks of wild turkeys roaming the woodlands, so it was easy for me to imagine the peacock taking over the leadership of a turkey flock. Male turkeys strut, show off their fan-shaped tails to attract females. The dominant male has first pick. The peacock, I imagined, with his fabulous, feathered train, would outdo common turkeys, be the equivalent of a rock star among female turkeys.

This was an early poem, written before I fully realized that literary journals don't usually publish "light verse," simple humor—it was rejected seven times.

The poem was finally published by Kelsay Books as part of the *Midwest Medley* collection in 2018, also later accepted for the 2023 edition of the *Wisconsin Fellowship of Poets Calendar*. The calendar theme for that year is "The Mythos of Wisconsin." *Mythos* defined as a set of beliefs or exaggerations found in a particular group or culture, is a subject that lends itself to "light" or humorous verse.

The title of the poem plays into the "Wisconsin mythos" idea—you can see strange things in Wisconsin. A peacock that takes over a flock of wild turkeys seemed to fit the theme. I'll keep an eye out for blue-feathered turkey chicks—you never know.

Close Encounters: I Met Lassie on the Stage of the Oriental Theater in Chicago

My mother took me to see Lassie, the film star, live on a Chicago Loop stage. The trainer called for volunteers—I sprinted up, beat out another contender, and Lassie extended her paw to me, sometime in the mid-1950s.

In the late 1960s, I stood near, almost touching, nine-times-wed Zsa Zsa Gabor rolling dice at a casino in Vegas. TV host Ed Sullivan and I, at neighboring tables in the lounge of the Sands Hotel, watched a performer play the marimba.

One cold day in '88, I shook hands with Bush 41 in a Green Bay airport hangar. He was on the campaign trail and came there to meet me, solicit my vote and pose for a photo, with officials who showed up to greet us.

I talked with Nick Charles of CNN, sexiest sports anchor of the 1990s. We met in an Atlanta import shop, chatted about foreign travel. Our eyes locked, filled with lust and hunger, as we ogled the same Persian carpet.

It was late October of '99 when I attended a forum in Dresden. There, at a conference cocktail bash, I encountered Umberto Eco. He wrote me a note on my seminar program and the evening closed with a post-modern ending.

The century morphed into the Twenty-First, when, on a Hawaiian thoroughfare, an unmistakable pair strolled ahead of me. It was "Dog the Bounty Hunter" and his partner Beth, stars of the *A&E* reality show.

The year was 2015 and the crowds hadn't stopped—another president was following me. Jimmy Carter and I both had a poem published in the same anthology, our words just a few pages apart.

I'm not sure I can tolerate all these people stalking me. Soon they'll plead for autographs, and I'll need a paid agent. Celebrities clamoring for my consideration—akin to a paparazzi invasion—is flagrant occupation of my personal space. It's hell being famous.

I wrote this poem about "celebrity-sightings" in 2013 and began a seven-year effort to get it published. The poem was rejected a total of twelve times before finally being accepted for the *Poeming Pigeon Pop Culture Issue,* 2020—sometimes you just have to wait for the one right opportunity.

Humorous poetry can be a hard sell. Publishers often see it as frivolous, although *satire,* humorous but biting, makes a point that often targets political or societal issues. The reader is not certain what is truth and what is only in the imagination of the author or narrator.

Note: The line in stanza five, "a post-modern ending," relates to Umberto Eco, author of the Postmodern Period (Post WW II), a Pop Culture icon known for *The Name of the Rose,* a 1980 novel and 1986 film. Eco explained his writing as a search for hyperreality, for the world of "the Absolute Fake." He questioned the meaning of truth from all perspectives: theological, historical, philosophical, scholarly. He did "write me a note on my seminar program"—his autograph, which I asked him for . . .

Postmodern literature relies on irony, unreliable narrators, impossible plots, parody, and it mixes humor with dark events.

Distress Signal: Growing Tomatoes Upside Down

Nature teaches more than she preaches
—John Burroughs

The Topsy Turvy Upside Down Tomato Planter
a gadget offered on eBay and Amazon,
available at Walmart, Best Buy and Lowes,
      also "Seen on TV"—
promises bigger and better tomatoes,
an earlier crop, avoids the backbreaking work
of growing them right-side-up.
Cutworms and ground fungus won't appear
      when you grow upside-down tomatoes.

Satisfied buyers praise upside-down planting
for growing splendid tomatoes in limited spaces—
unshaded places and sun-drenched porches
      perfect to nurture upside-down tomatoes.
Raised in the conventional way,
tomatoes need staking to keep stems from breaking,
a condition that arises from weight.
Cherry tomatoes diminish problems, do well enough
      grown right-side-up.

There's a drawback to raising inverted tomatoes.
Plants signal distress, struggle upward,
stems make U-turns, reach for the sky—
      roots crawl out of the pot,
stretch toward the earth, pursue a downward direction.
Efforts to change them . . . .
      like trying to train willful children.

A gardening device called an "upside down tomato planter" was widely advertised in 2020 when this was written. "Distress Signal" was rejected by three journals before *Your Daily Poem* accepted it.

There is a metaphor hiding in the poem's title: according to the U.S. Flag Code, flying a flag upside-down is a distress signal. As we learn, upside-down tomatoes are suffering distress as they struggle upward.

Positive feedback from readers is the most gratifying aspect of writing poetry. Comments by readers of YDP who recognized that many of us are upside-down tomatoes, included:

"I have never heard of growing upside-down tomatoes before, but your description of it is great, as is your connection of it to larger life issues!"

"The turn in the last stanza is metaphorical—and powerful. We do what we need to do to make ourselves be what we are."

Futile Struggle: Salute to the Rural Mailbox

WANTED:
Young, skinny, wiry fellows not over eighteen.
Must be expert riders, willing to risk death daily.
Orphans preferred
              —Pony Express recruitment ad

Our mailbox is new, replaced the one flattened
by juiced-up young men, midnight riding—
unaware that willful damage is a federal offense,
with fines or imprisonment possible.
If you leave the scene of a mailbox collision,
you can be prosecuted for "hit and run."

Violators don't discriminate by style or color,
target post or pedestal mounted.
Brave as riders for the *Pony Express,*
boxes stand on less traveled roads,
vulnerable, invisible to their owners,
susceptible to attacks from baseball bats.

Our latest protector of postal material,
fresh from the shelves of the *Fleet Farm* store,
stands at the road, plain and brave—
only eighteen days out, but already wounded
when the county snowplow hurled its load.

This is a bit of country nostalgia, a situation not always known to city dwellers, an autobiographical poem with an ironic, but true, ending. Through the years we have had mailboxes smashed, bashed, thrown into the nearby river, but this was the first time our county road crew was to blame.

The poem didn't win anything in a contest except some appreciated encouragement from an editor: *"We did want to note that we were particularly drawn to 'Futile Struggle' and hope to see more work from you in the future."*

"Futile Struggle" was eventually published in 2018 in the *Midwest Medley* collection and also by *Your Daily Poem,* where it was popular with readers who made numerous comments:

"Nostalgic piece, reminding me of similar events among folks I have known."
"Let's hear it for lonely mailboxes! Well done."
"Country mailboxes don't stand a chance. Love your poem!"

"We bring the mailbox inside every day after mail delivery and return it to its post every morning!"
"As a product of central Illinois' farm country, I'm with you all the way on the perils of life as a roadside mailbox!"

"Unusual subject . . . making for an outstanding poem!"
"Great poem. Brought back memories!!"
"Cute poem with that nice, unexpected twist at the end via the county snowplow."

"Funny. The poor openly, assaultable mailbox."
"Love the juiced-up line!"
"My brother and a couple of friends blew up a few mailboxes with firecrackers when he was young."

Lockdown Is Frying My Brain

Being locked down during this pandemic—time crawling by, no hugs from friends—has led to questions I've never had time to ask. How intelligent are pigs? Do lobsters mate for life? What about left-swirling snail shells?

Pigs are smarter than other domestic animals, outshine three-year-old children on cognition tests. Experts say they're more trainable than dogs—definitely more so than cats—but *trainable* doesn't equal *intelligent*.

Never knew about the sex-life of lobsters; I read that the males are promiscuous—have a monogamous bond lasting about two weeks—behavior similar to that of some humans.

A male snail with a left-swirling shell finds it difficult, I read, to mate with the typical right-swirling lady, whose genitals are on the opposite side of her head—decided not to pursue it further.

Can Wookies become Jedi? Simple answer: yes, but it's uncommon. And how old is Chewbacca in human years? The fictional, hirsute, humanoid alien, based on orangutans and lemurs, is currently 234 years old. . . . . had enough?

People don't usually find humor in a pandemic—more likely to center on losing loved ones, or empty streets. This purely fun piece made me laugh all the while I was writing it—perhaps an inappropriate response to a serious situation, or just that "Postmodern" influence.

I always heard that pigs were highly intelligent, but don't remember where or why I came across the other information in the poem. I just know I felt inspired to incorporate it in a poem. "Lockdown" was rejected the first time it was sent out.

The Brits manage to see humor in many serious situations—if you're old enough, think Monty Python pushing the boundaries of what was acceptable. I thought this poem might have good luck with a British publication.

I submitted it to the *COVID-19 Writing Competition* sponsored by *Dissonance Magazine,* located in the U.K. The poem was short-listed, not the top winner, but one of the five finalists published in December of 2020. I considered being a finalist a win.

Waiting for Janis Joplin

When you're old and passing time, listening over and over to Andrea Bocelli singing *Time to Say Goodbye* on YouTube and drinking third-rate cabernet, or listening—at four in the morning—to Mongolian throat songs that sound like groans from the halls of Hell—you can't help thinking about death.

What about my funeral song—I like *Me and Bobby McGee, "freedom's just another word . . ."* but I've heard enough goodbyes, let somebody else pick the music—think I'll buy chandelier earrings, like the sparkly ones worn by divas who sing with Bocelli. Now is the time to indulge—there's *"nothin' left to lose."*

I'll improve my mind, they say it's never too late—read acclaimed novels, like *The Plague,* about moral and allegorical pestilence that sweeps a city—best read, I hear, as metaphor, suited to the present on every level—want to find out if the rats in the building are the same as the ones we have in "the houses."

I'll need more books to read. *Love in the Time of Cholera* or maybe *One Hundred Years of Solitude,* sound about right.

The success of "Lockdown is Frying my Brain" led me to submit "Waiting for Janis Joplin" to a contest. The poem never mentions the covid pandemic or politics but alludes to both subjects.

Originally written in the early days of the pandemic, it was strictly for fun, not intended for submission, just an amusing distraction for friends who enjoyed sharing a laugh. It received a "thumbs-up" from all of them. I "tuned it up," submitted it unsuccessfully, to five journals. (My friends obviously didn't have the same expertise as those editors.)

I was intending to send something to the annual *Hal Prize for Poetry, 2022,* sponsored by *Peninsula Pulse,* a Door County, Wisconsin, newspaper, but my "Deadline-reminder List" was somehow misplaced (I confess, I forgot about it), not discovered until the day of the deadline. I didn't have time to fine-tune the poem I was originally planning to submit, so I sent five-time loser, "Janis" back into competition.

I don't usually enter poetry contests unless they are free or have minimal entry fees. This one was five dollars. I hated to miss an opportunity, even though I knew winning anything was a longshot. Readership of the *Peninsula Pulse* publications is high and Door County is an "artsy" place, so poetic participation was likely to be heavy. The three top winners of the *Hal Prize* and several Honorable Mention choices would receive publication in the new literary journal, *Peninsula Pulse 8142 Review.* The top three winners would receive cash prizes as well.

To my delight, "Waiting for Janis Joplin" cut through the preliminaries and received "finalist" status, then went on to win Third Place.

PART V

Home & Neighborhood
Coming & Going

*They all stay with us,
family and places, home and neighborhood*

Exiled

I dreamed of returning home that first spring.

Walking along the river last summer,
under burnished moonlight,
I saw reflections of alien scenery
and missed home even more.

In autumn, my coat was drenched with tears.
When snowflakes cover me, I will still be here—
alone, and longing for home.

This poem, "Exiled," written early in my poetry venture, was well received by my poetry coach: *"This is a powerful poem! . . . I really like the simple, straightforward ending here, reminds me of Chinese poetry."*

It was rejected six times during the first year and two more times the next year, a grand total of eight rejections. One of the editors did send words of encouragement, *"I admired most 'Exile,' which captures some of the tone of the T'ang Dynasty Chinese poets."* Two years after it was written, *Mused Online Journal* published it.

My writing was never consciously inspired by Chinese poetry, but influential things are not always immediately recognized. It was, whether or not I realized it at the time, my last university project which involved Chinese painting and poetry that sparked my interest in writing poetry of my own.

Islands

There's a desolate stretch of highway
between two stop signs
and two corner bars
—bright islands in night-dark waters—
twenty miles from anywhere.

Sun-baked farmers in beat-up seed caps*
patronize both places—laugh,
repeat old stories, tell old news,
talk about the weather, guess
how many deer roam the back forty.

A disillusioned woman, restless and lonely,
looks for an evening companion,
a tryst in the parking lot.
Somebody's kids eat French fries,
play arcade games in an alcove off the bar.

A grizzled regular, lank-haired,
spare and hollow-eyed, stares at the TV,
locked in self-imposed silence—
lives nearby in quiet desperation, exiled
from the present, nowhere else to go.

Lighted ports in evening seas ease
more than weary bodies
—keep more than thirst at bay—
halfway between somewhere
and nowhere.

seed salesmen often give farmers caps bearing their company logo.

"Islands" was rejected by three literary journals and an anthology of "bar poems" (which I was sure would accept my "bar poem" based on a variety of neighborhood watering holes).

In 2017, on the fifth try, two years after it was written, "Islands" was not only published, but selected to receive the Editor's Choice Award from *Waypoints*, a literature and art journal. The editor wrote this encouraging note:

"A lot of the poems I receive, though well-written, describe a place without including critical elements of the experience in that place. I select poems that are multi-dimensional. 'Islands' speaks not only to the place, but to time and humanity in that place. I think that your poem does this exceptionally well."

It was also published in my 2018 collection, *Midwest Medley* and the *Wisconsin Fellowship of Poets* calendar for 2020 which had the theme, "Going Places."

Homage to Art: Abstract and Conceptual

To my old neighbor, Hemmy Ness

Hemmy saw beauty in porcelain fixtures
of a certain cerulean hue.
He saw it in his rainbow roof shingles
patterned like quilts on Victorian beds.

He heard beauty in music, teased
from an old violin, songs bringing tears
to his eyes and pain to the ears of his guests
when he played in the bathroom—
the acoustics were better there, he said.

But his passion was rusted machinery
and metal objects of varied design,
parts of old Fords and worn-out Chevys
piled high in the side yard,
treasures, which he explained:

"There's a dinosaur, a zebra, a boy and
his dog, a ship as slick as ever sailed the seas.
And wait 'til you see them in winter,
painted all white with new-fallen snow."

Midwest Prairie Review accepted "Homage to Art" after four other journals refused this recollection of an old neighbor. The editor wrote:

"We received hundreds of submissions. Your material rose to the top of our files with the journal's editorial board agreeing that your material best embodied the spirit and theme for this issue."

The poem also appears in my collection, *Midwest Medley* (Kelsay Books, 2018).

The artist in me concluded that Hemmy had an unwitting eye for art and design. His aesthetic appreciation of the scrap heaps that filled his yard and his uncommon home decorating choices seemed akin to the art world's high regard for the abstract and conceptual.

Hemmy's violin music was equally abstract and a true experience for the listeners. He sat in the bathroom, perched on the bright blue, non-functioning toilet (in four years, he had never gotten around to putting in a septic system), and while tears streamed down his cheeks, Hemmy played songs that all sounded alike.

I treasure these memories of someone who so innocently enjoyed the private haven he had created.

Lumber Business

We sat on the sofa, visiting with Uncle Alvin—
silver-haired, past eighty, still a dapper dresser,
a ladies' man, outlived two wives
—looking for number three—
always thought of himself as successful,
ran a logging crew like his immigrant father.

Hoped his business would improve next year,
and talked of current problems—
white pine shortages in the Great Lakes states,
grasshoppers eating crops in the heartland,
mechanical tractors replacing work horses.

He stood, asked our names as he walked
toward the window, embraced the view outside
—smiled when a shapely nurse entered—
then gestured toward the stacks of lumber
only he could see.

The main character in this poem, based on a relative who was in an assisted living facility, is a universal type. Elderly, no longer mentally living in the present, he is back in the days when mechanical tractors were replacing work horses, but still has "an eye for the ladies."

Uncle Alvin exists on many family trees, but apparently didn't make an impression on any one of the seven journal editors who turned down the poem. It did, however, resonate with general readers on social media when it appeared there.

Accepted for the *Wisconsin Fellowship of Poets 2019 Calendar,* with the theme of "Wisconsin People," it was also published in the *Midwest Medley* collection (Kelsay Books).

Remembering Small Times

Some days I recall
sweet and fierce small times,
grounded in the ordinary—

the dog, not bought for me,
but mine, nonetheless—
ninety pounds of blackness
standing by my side,
shoulders and legs stiffly erect,
resonant rumble in his throat
when strangers came to the door—

a downy white cat, not mine either,
sat at my feet
in companionable silence
while I worked
at the timeworn desk—

I buried him wrapped in
my pink baby blanket.

Another of my first-year pieces, "Remembering Small Times" was only rejected twice before being accepted by *Peninsula Pulse*. My poetry coach commented:

"Awwww! Effective poem! I like the repetition of 'not mine' when they clearly are very much yours. Powerful last image."

When I compiled *Midwest Medley,* in 2018, I included this. Some things are never forgotten, still have the power, years later, to tug at your heart. I've had many pets since then, loved them all, sometimes still choke up when remembering each one.

Not everyone, however, including editors, or should I say, especially most editors, wants to read about deceased pets or dead deer along the road. I have seen warnings in submission guidelines about such subjects. Submit them at your own peril.

Door County Picnic

We bought cabernet and crackers,
locally smoked whitefish
wrapped in yesterday's news,
from a shop with outdoor tables
overlooking the bay.

I set the table with plastic wine glasses,
held one up in an unconscious gesture.
The clear plastic caught sunlight,
showcased tints and shades
pierced by arcs of color—

My husband twirled his glass
too fast to see the magic.
I looked again, still saw rainbows
spilling a million hues.
I motioned him to slow down.
We didn't need fine crystal
to see the play of light.

"Door County Picnic" is another one of those little "slice of life" poems that are born of small moments, recalling the poet's quiet times—here, the delightful memory of a picnic on the Lake Michigan shore, where sunlight made rainbows that streamed through plastic wine glasses.

The poem was rejected twice before *Midwest Review* published it. The journal interprets the wide spectrum of life in the Midwest and points out that the Midwest is also a state of mind, a description that surely defines this poem. "Door County Picnic" was also published in the *Midwest Medley* collection.

Family Legacy

I recall my mother's mantra,
her frequent refrain when I was a child:
like her mother who died at thirty-nine,
she wouldn't make it to forty.

Had my doomed parent survived,
she would have passed a century next month,
but ninety-four years and a half,
was all she managed to last.

"Family Legacy," based on a youthful recollection, has caused some readers to say how awful it must have been for a child to hear her mother say such things. But I heard it so often that I became desensitized, always felt she would probably live to be a hundred. She came close.

From a technical point, my writing coach was complimentary about the use of *irony* and *slant rhyme,* a type of rhyme with words that have similar, but not identical sounds, also called *near* rhyme. She said:

"I like the irony here! Like the slant rhyme too, of half and last."

One of the most influential poets of the 19th century, Emily Dickinson is famous for using *slant rhyme*. She relied on it rather than the typical *exact rhyme* schemes of her time.

Irony occurs when a person says or does something that departs from what we expect them to say or do, as in the narrator's ironic line, "ninety-four years and a half, was all she managed to last" instead, for example, of something similar to "in spite of her fears, she lived to be almost a hundred."

After three rejections, *Poetry Quarterly* accepted this first-year piece, with a note from the editor:

"Exactly, perfection here, cadence, language, message, flavor, everything."—one of those brief but powerful encouragements so appreciated, especially by a beginner. "Family Legacy" was also included in the 2018 *Midwest Medley* manuscript.

Aunt Mae's Player Piano

It sat in an alcove off the parlor
in Great-aunt Mae's house,
came alive on Friday nights.

Mae, my mother, her cousins and I,
gathered 'round the archaic upright,
pumped the pedal and sang old songs
from Aunt Mae's younger days.

Ebony and ivory keys
danced without help from human fingers.
Rotating rolls, yellowed by time,
peppered with cryptic perforations,
resonated with ragtime
and operetta music.

Aunt Mae had a peculiar voice,
warbled louder than everyone else,
reminded me of a yodel—
When we sang *The Desert Song,*
she closed her eyes and sinuously swayed.
Transported to Morocco,
Mae became Myrna Loy.*

I can feel the grit of the desert
on certain Friday nights.
I see camels with riders crossing the dunes
and hear echoes of a little girl singing—
*"My desert is waiting,
dear, come there with me . . ."*

---

* *Actress Myrna Loy appeared in the 1929 film version of Sigmund Romberg's operetta,* The Desert Song.

"Aunt Mae's Player Piano" was published in *Your Daily Poem* and in the *Midwest Medley* collection (Kelsay Books) after being rejected by two literary journals. It struck a chord with YDP readers. To get this type of feedback is reason enough to write poetry. A few of the comments included:

"I played most of the great jazz, popular, and even some concert pianists during the dark ending days of World War II."

"Powerful memories emerged from reading this poem today."

"This reminds me of my grandparents pianola in New Zealand and the magic of the perforated paper slowly rolling and producing music from the past."

"I like the way we meet the relatives in this piece."

"What a fun poem, and what wonderful memories!"

"The final verse is my favorite and I like the way the poem builds up to it. A very visual poem."

"Unique and compelling, nicely done, the desert is calling!"

"I love this narrative nostalgia poem about a player piano bringing families together, transporting them to another land, another time."

"We have a player piano given to me by an aunt so this poem is dear to me."

BTW, years later I actually made it to Morocco, crossed the dunes on a camel, and I swear, heard the strains of a familiar melody floating over "the grit of the desert."

Ahead of Schedule

Children are a gift
—a gift you can't keep—
one you hold a single season.

We prepared for the moment
—a moment, in some far tomorrow—
when you would be gone.

We just didn't think
tomorrow would happen
—so fast.

"Ahead of Schedule" is a poem for all of the young parents who sometimes feel overwhelmed, feel it will be a relief when the children grow up. That's understandable, but oh, how those years quickly pass us, the children are gone, and somehow, we are old.

The poem was only rejected once before being published by *Mused* and then re-published in the *Midwest Medley* collection. *Your Daily Poem,* where it received much-appreciated comments from readers, also published it:

*"This made me smile,
but it is an arrow through the heart nonetheless."*

"This poem is a gift, Patricia. Such a deep 'feeling' poem."

"I admire the depth of its simplicity. I am always amazed at how a good poet can distill a big truth into a few lines. Ms. Williams has certainly accomplished that with this poem."

Missing Home

Alone in a faraway place
with no one to share thoughts
and no one to share mutual memories,
despondency flourishes.

Missing the familiar,
I look at the moon and feel comforted,
knowing my loved ones
see the same light overhead.

"Missing Home," written in 2013, was influenced by my interest in Chinese poetry. The inspiration came while I was away from home, participating in a week-long poetry workshop. That workshop gave me needed direction as a beginning poet.

"Missing Home" was rejected by one journal, then was published in the *Wisconsin Fellowship of Poets 2016 Calendar* which had the theme, "Shadows and Reflections."

"Missing Home" was accepted in 2016 by *Your Daily Poem,* with favorable comments from readers:

"I've felt those feelings." "Beautifully stated." "I love this!"

"The same sun shines on all, warming the heart." "Lovely."

"Beautiful sentiment." "This is simply beautiful."

All Hail Wausau, Wisconsin

Experts on weather describe four seasons,
but here, snow may fall in every month, except July,
and that's a historical fact.
Yes, you shovel, yes, you plow—all over Wausau,
but there's "city living with the country just minutes away."

Wear a jacket filled with down, celebrate sun,
but tolerate overcast days with style and grace,
fish through holes in ice-covered lakes, play ice hockey,
ride snowmobiles (those motorcycles on snow)—in Wausau,
where there's "city living with the country just minutes away."

The "sweeping" sport called curling has a history here
since the early 1900s, over a hundred years ago.
Back then, in fact, rocks were slid on the frozen river
(like shuffleboard on ice)—around Wausau,
where it's "city living with the country just minutes away."

This city, a little east of the middle of Wisconsin's largest county,
provides the world's best place for growing ginseng,
a medicinal root, farmed close to here.
There's more than cheese and snow, brats and beer—near Wausau.
Nice to have "city living with the country just minutes away."

All hail historic Grand Theater, the famed 400 Block, old
Milwaukee Road depot, "Birds in Art" at the Woodson Museum.
All hail world-class lumber and paper trades, autumns
of red and gold, and so much more to know—about Wausau.
It's "city living with the country just minutes away."

Although this poem is about a specific city, probably unfamiliar to many readers, it is in the spirit, if not the details, of the "hometown" that many can identify with.

"All Hail Wausau, Wisconsin" is an ode, a poem that addresses and praises or glorifies a person, place, thing, event or idea; it celebrates the worth or influence of something. John Keats's poem, "Ode on a Grecian Urn" describes the timelessness of art, Shelley's "Ode to the West Wind" addresses nature's strength.

Contemporary odes also celebrate the unexpected, praise the hidden worth of mundane things, like Pablo Neruda's "Ode to My Socks" or "Ode to a Large Tuna in the Market."

One of many place names with origins in a Native American language, *wau-sau* is an Ojibwe word meaning "faraway place" or "distance." The poem was written for a competition sponsored by the *Central Wisconsin Book Festival,* in celebration of the city's 150-year history. This was one of twenty-four poems chosen to be placed on posters and hung in storefronts for a poetry walk during September 2022.

My inspiration came from first-hand acquaintance with the city of Wausau, located "just up the road" from my house, almost "in my backyard," several "country miles" away (maybe fifty?).

A historical, somewhat tangential end note on country miles:

The oldest reference to a country mile was published in 1829 in Frederick de Kruger's poem, *The Villager's Tale*: "Twas long indeed, a country mile." Miles in cities mean something different than country miles. Country roads are seldom straight, thus they require longer travel time than travelers might expect.

The account of my poetry adventure has indeed been several country miles long, with many twists, turns and detours along the way. I hope you enjoyed riding along.

About the Author

Life and poetry are always subject to revision.

Patricia Williams, originally from the Chicago area, began writing poetry in 2013 after retiring from a teaching career in Art and Design. She taught in the Wisconsin K-12 school system, then, for 27 years, taught at the University of Wisconsin - Stevens Point. Pat and her husband live in the Wisconsin countryside, eight miles from Iola, a village of 1,300, and 25 miles from any place larger.

Her poetry appears in literary journals and anthologies and was chosen for several painting and poetry collaborations. She has a chapbook, *The Portside of Shadows: Poems of Travel* (Finishing Line Press) and an award-winning collection, *Midwest Medley: Places & People, Wild Things & Weather* (Kelsay Books) which the *Wisconsin Library Association* designated "Outstanding Achievement in Poetry for 2018."

Pat was nominated for the *Pushcart Prize* and *Best-of-the-Net* award, placed for the *Kay Saunders Emerging Poet* award and the *Hal Prize*. One of her poems is embedded in the Main Street sidewalks of the city of Waupaca, Wisconsin. She has read her work in coffee shops, bars, libraries, auditoriums, at outdoor gatherings and dinner parties—any place where people are willing to listen.

Patricia's books can be purchased on amazon.com or from the publishers:

The Portside of Shadows: Poems of Travel Finishing Line Press:
https://www.finishinglinepress.com/product/the-port-side-of-shadows-by-patricia-williams/

Midwest Medley: Places & People, Wild Things & Weather
Kelsay Books: https://kelsaybooks.com/products/midwest-medley-places-people-wild-things-weather

www.ingramcontent.com/pod-product-compliance
Lightning Source LLC
Chambersburg PA
CBHW022013160426
43197CB00007B/412